WITHDRAWN
University of
Illinois Library
at Urbana-Champaign

Economics
and Operational Research

Topics in Operational Research

Since the end of the Second World War, studies in the field of Management Sciences and Operational Research have developed at an extraordinary speed, and have gained in width and depth.

The present series of books on 'Topics in Operational Research' contains contributions from authors who have special expertise in this field. There exist, of course, excellent texts on the theoretical background, but this series fulfils a need for detailed descriptions of simple numerical or algebraic techniques, and for reports on practical experience with these techniques, useful to managers and executives in many branches of social, commercial and industrial activity. Knowledge of such techniques will be spread more widely by the publication of these monographs, and further development stimulated thereby.

The texts are written in such a way that little, if any, advanced knowledge from any branch of science will be required of the reader and no mathematical knowledge beyond A-level G.C.E. or O.N.C.

The various books in the series should thus be of interest not only to management and engineering personnel, but also to teachers in the later forms in schools, and in colleges, as suggestions for possible syllabuses for introductory courses and as sources of interesting problems and examples.

S. VAJDA

Economics
and Operational Research

M. H. BEILBY

Department of Transportation and Environmental Planning,
The University of Birmingham, England

ACADEMIC PRESS, INC.   New York   San Francisco
A Subsidiary of Harcourt Brace Jovanovich, Publishers
1976

First published in Great Britain by
Sir Isaac Pitman & Sons Limited

Published in the United States and Canada by
Academic Press Inc. 1976

© M. H. Beilby 1975

Library of Congress Catalog Card Number 75-34845

ISBN 0-12-085750-2

All rights reserved. No part of this publication may be reproduced, stored in a retrieval system, or transmitted, in any form or by any means, electronic, mechanical, photocopying, recording and/or otherwise, without the prior permission of the publishers.

Text set in 10/11 pt. Monotype Times, printed by letterpress, and bound in Great Britain at The Pitman Press, Bath

Preface

Operational research has developed as a collection of techniques for solving specific management problems, while economics is concerned with the more general question of the organization of human and material resources. A link between the subject areas provides a powerful analytic tool, and this book explores the possible connections by concentrating on the interpretations of management decisions at different levels in the economy.

Essentially operational research involves building a mathematical model. It relies on suitably breaking down a situation to its basic components so that the effects of decisions can be accurately reconstructed. An obvious starting point for economic problems is to separate out consumption and production, and build a framework round each of them independently. Hence the early chapters 2, 3 and 4 concentrate on describing how consumers manage their own budgets and manufacturers select their production processes. With these building blocks established it is then possible to move on and in chapter 5 investigate generally how consumers and producers react to each other.

In the chapters that follow the principles developed are applied to specific planning problems. One of these is the transportation of goods and people through busy road networks. Besides being topical, it touches on a number of interesting points, the efficiency attained through central planning, the control of congestion that arises through decentralization, and the construction of an overall planning model. In these broad terms transportation represents a major problem for community life, and experience in that area provides a useful case study. This should become apparent in chapters 6, 7 and 8.

Chapter 9 looks at some aspects of national planning. The collection of all consumers and producers makes up one large economic system which appears to lumber along at its own pace usually to the consternation of the government. There is a great deal of literature devoted to the question of why it behaves as it does and how future situations might be controlled by careful planning. There is only room in this book to introduce the field but, in so doing, it is possible to show some of the power of the combination of operational research and economics.

In a smiliar way the closing chapter provides a glimpse at another large subject area. Planning over several time periods is one step more complicated than the problems in the rest of the book and there is an increasing amount written about techniques that have been specially designed to cope. All that can be done is to indicate some developments and leave more detailed study to a stage beyond this mere introduction.

Two stumbling blocks for someone meeting the subjects of operational research and economics for the first time are inevitably the mathematical notation and the economic jargon. These obstacles cannot be avoided altogether but, in order to help, the commonly used symbols and terms are explained in the text and in a mathematical appendix. Those in the text are printed in italics and can be cross-referenced through the index at the back of the book, and pointers to explanations in the appendix are provided by the letter A followed by the number of the appropriate section. A second appendix supplies a concise statement of mathematical programming problems and their associated properties.

Generally, the discussions are aimed at a readership which is familiar with some basic mathematics. It is hard to point to any minimum standard, but much of the material in the book relies on an understanding of differentiation of functions of several variables. This falls well within the mathematical content that is included in most undergraduate courses in the social, pure and applied sciences, and in engineering.

There is a current tendency towards teaching such general topics as management, transportation, resource allocation and urban and regional planning through multidisciplinary courses at graduate or post-experience level. It is hoped that this book will provide a means of linking theories that otherwise are taught and remain separate in peoples' minds. In addition it should be of interest to those who, in a

Preface vii

more general way, wish to use economics and mathematics together as an analytical tool. As such it should demonstrate to them how economic theory can be expressed and mathematics applied.

Much help has been received in bringing the book together and, although any errors remain the responsibility of the author, the particular advice and comment of Professor S. Vajda and Mr J. P. Hanlon is acknowledged. Also the burden of typing manuscripts has been taken up by many willing hands amongst which are those of Mrs D. Vick. It is hoped that the words that have been assembled provide interest for the reader.

Birmingham, M.H.B.
August, 1974

Contents

Preface · v

1 Introduction · 1

2 Consumer Behaviour · 4
2.1 Description of Tastes and Preferences
2.2 Basic Assumptions
2.3 A Two-good Example
2.4 A General Model of Demand
2.5 A Generalized Model of Consumer Behaviour
2.6 A Time Allocation Model

3 Production Planning · 25
3.1 Meeting a Production Target
3.2 Activity Analysis
3.3 Searching for Improvement
3.4 The Optimal Position

4 Computation and Valuation · 42
4.1 The Simplex Method
4.2 Derivation of the Supply Curve
4.3 Value at the Margin
4.4 A Decomposition Algorithm

5 Behaviour of the Firm · 65
5.1 Economic Models of the Firm
5.2 Perfect Competition
5.3 Non-linearities; Variable Returns to Scale and Monopolies
5.4 Market Games
5.5 Alternative Objectives

6	**Transport Planning**	87
	6.1 The Transportation Problem	
	6.2 The Interpretation of Shadow Costs	
	6.3 Problems of Traffic Planning	
	6.4 Application to Urban Planning Problems	
7	**Traffic Control**	106
	7.1 A Bid System	
	7.2 A Ballot System	
	7.3 Congestion of Road Space	
	7.4 Choice of Time of Travel	
8	**Models of Location**	123
	8.1 Location and Economic Rent	
	8.2 Location of Industrial Activity within a Region	
	8.3 Distribution of Residential Activity	
	8.4 A Model of Industrial Location and Trade between Regions	
9	**Linear Techniques and the Economy**	137
	9.1 A Complete Productive System	
	9.2 Perfectly Competitive Equilibrium	
	9.3 Input–Output Analysis	
10	**Consideration of Time**	151
	10.1 Consumer Behaviour	
	10.2 Production Planning	
	10.3 Growth in the Economy	

References and Further Reading   157

Appendix A: Mathematical Notes   160

Appendix B: Mathematical Programming: Summary   167

Index   171

1 Introduction

From an historical point of view there would seem to be little reason to bring together the subjects of economics and operational research. Economics has its origin in the Greek work for 'housekeeping' and has developed to be concerned with the management of the financial affairs of a nation. This has involved consideration both of its internal book-keeping and its standing in the distribution of world resources. Until the 19th century the home economy was very simple with consumption of goods that were produced directly on the land or from raw materials with relatively primitive machinery. Economic debate mainly centred around foreign trade and the way in which government decisions affected the activities of merchants. It was only in the 19th century that the coming of the Industrial Revolution to Britain introduced an upsurge of manufacturing which relied on capital equipment and employment of labour on an organized basis. This made the economy into an object of some substance and signalled the beginning of new interest in its management. It also has provided an established position for the economics of production and, while political issues are still dominated by concern in financial terms about international trade, there is now a well-recognized addition to the list of national resources, productive capacity.

Operational research (or 'operations research' as it is referred to in the United States) sprang up comparatively recently as a management tool for use in large organizations where there is not necessarily any form of money exchange. It has been concerned with the application of mathematical methods to specific planning problems such as the organization of logistic support for large-scale military operations. The importance of this sort of work started the development of techniques during the Second World War and this has since led to applications throughout industry. In contrast to the generalization common in economics, the methods are appropriate for the solution of very narrowly defined problems.

The difference in emphasis provides a good reason for bringing the two approaches together. They complement each other in a wide range of applied problems. Particularly in the areas of consumption, production and resource allocation it is possible to give economics the task of identifying planning objectives and hence defining which outcomes are preferable in a specific situation. Operational research then provides a basis for formulating the problem and a set of methods by which the 'best' solution can be evaluated. In fact, the parts played by the two subjects become closely interlinked and it is often difficult to draw a line between them.

In an attempt to identify the subject areas at least at the outset, their definitions can be narrowed. For the purposes of this book economics is taken to be concerned with the allocation of resources in a world organized through a system of exchange of goods between individuals. The emphasis is thus taken away from the financial transactions mentioned above and placed on the detail of consumption and production of goods, and the scarcity of resources from which they are made. This could be described as a *microscopic* rather than a *macroscopic* approach; the object of study is the behaviour of people and organizations that in total make up the economy, instead of the apparent relationship between such aggregate quantities as employment levels or trade balances which themselves influence government policy. The argument is that the microscopic behaviour will give an insight into decision-making within business organizations, investment planning in the community, and organization of resources in the whole productive economy.

The formulation of problems will follow a specific framework. The appropriate branch of mathematics that helps do this is *mathematical programming*. It has already found a wide application to general operational research problems and provides an established theoretical background for economic problems. Quite simply, the subject itself concentrates on finding the maximum or minimum value that a given mathematical function can take while the values of its variables obey certain constraints (A1, A2, A3). The particular advantage of adopting this for a framework for tackling economic problems is that it can be applied to questions of optimization for which there will then be techniques available to search for actual solutions. Therefore, at the start, the economic analysis will aim at reducing a problem to the specific mathematical programming format which, once achieved, indicates what is required to obtain the final solution. The format is described in detail in Appendix B.

It could be said that the mathematical framework makes up a *model*, an abstraction from a real situation which still retains some important features. There are usually two ways in which this can be useful, for *explanation* or for *prediction*. In the first case, it explains the relationships and hence helps the understanding of a situation for which judgements have to be made about future policy. In the second, it attempts to reconstruct values and aims at predicting what would

Introduction 3

happen if a given course of action were adopted. These two approaches echo closely the distinction between *normative* and *positive* economics which ask the questions 'what ought to be?' and 'what will be if...?' respectively. As such they allow planning to be concerned either with the wisdom of organizing society on the basis of such principles as 'free trade' or 'decentralization', or with the outcome of particular decisions such as 'to increase or not to increase by 5 per cent the price of travel by public transport'. This is equivalent to distinguishing between a mathematical approach to economics, where the thinking is kept in the abstract, and a statistical approach, where the models have to display some element of realism in the quantities involved. However it is expressed, though, the emphasis in the use of a model will be in either explanation or prediction and it is important to recall the methodology behind the building of the model when it is eventually applied to a real situation.

A feature of the models is that, to fit into a framework of mathematical programming, they involve optimization in some way or other. Typically the normative economic models look at the objectives of society as a whole. For example, a developing country would probably wish to strengthen its position by maximizing productive capacity and then, once it has achieved a prescribed level, change completely and aim towards some specific social goal. In contrast, the positive economic models usually include optimization in the behaviour of the participants. Thus consumer behaviour would be expected to hinge on an individual's getting the 'best' deal for himself, and production behaviour on earning the largest profit. As is seen in the early chapters, these behavioural aspects are relatively easy to isolate, based as they are on individual motivations. As the book proceeds, though, they become more interlinked with the broader concepts of perfect competition and efficiency that spread over the whole community and so play a large part in deciding how an overall target might be achieved.

2 Consumer Behaviour

A simple analysis of industrial activities would show that there are three basic processes, buying materials, production and selling the result. Much of the time one firm sells to another which in turn sells to another and so on along a chain of business negotiations. Ultimately a final product or service will meet a consumer market, and its success or failure monitored back along the line with a review of production targets and cost–price relationships. It could be said that the consumer calls the tune, with the whole business mechanism depending in the end on the tastes and preferences of the population. Certainly this is recognized commercially and a large amount of attention is being paid to market research. Then the information is sought on how potential customers might behave if offered different products at specific prices. This helps the manufacturer take planning decisions, particularly with respect to his marketing and sales targets.

Although the economy as a whole has a more complex interplay of activities than the individual firm, there is still a large part to be played by the population. As consumers of goods they will together determine the success or failure of businesses and hence cause shifts in investment between industries. In their further capacities as a work force and as part of a political system they will help shape policies for the operation of the complete economy. Clearly, then, from the point of view of planning in both private and public sectors, it would be desirable to know something of peoples' behaviour as consumers, workers and voters, and to carry out a market research exercise on all goods, work activities and political opinions. These three possibilities make up the province of the social sciences in general, and this chapter concentrates on the first exercise from a specifically practical point of view. Knowing that it must lead to an eventual framework for economic transactions, it looks at the consumer's expenditure pattern. The only part of his psychological or sociological make-up of interest is that which determines his attitude towards the quantity of goods he buys.

2.1 Description of Tastes and Preferences

To build a basis for a general theory of behaviour, consider a particular consumer placed in the unreal position of being offered the choice of consuming different selections of goods with no expenditure or other restriction at all. For example, forgetting the cost, which type of car would he chose from all those currently on the market? Which piece of meat would he prefer to eat from those on the butcher's slab? In such situations it would be expected that his own tastes and preferences would lead him to a decision.

To make the example more complicated, the consumer could be further offered the choice, say, between two packages of goods A and B, the first containing 1 lb of tea and ¼lb butter, and the second ⅛lb tea and ½lb butter. He might then prefer B. If he did, how would he choose between package A and yet another package, C, containing ¼lb tea and ⅛lb butter? It would be expected that the reduction in the quantity of tea from B to C would reduce its desirability, and, although the package C would not necessarily be as desirable as A, some other package containing a quantity of tea and ½lb butter would be. This type of comparison provides a basis by which an ordering can be placed on the desirability of packages, and a mechanism can be derived for drawing out those combinations between which the consumer is indifferent.

The comparisons are used to define consumer behaviour. Consider that n goods are presented to the consumer in a large number of different combinations of non-negative quantities $(x_1, x_2, \ldots x_n)$. It would then be possible to draw out a set of 'contours' through points between which the consumer was indifferent and effectively create a set of relationships (A4),

$$f(x_1, x_2, \ldots x_n) = \lambda$$

where λ is a constant value that identifies a 'contour'. By convention, if package A is preferred to package B, then the associated values of λ, λ_A and λ_B will be such that $\lambda_A > \lambda_B$ (A5).

The function f has become known as the *utility function*, and the contours usually referred to as *indifference curves*, or *surfaces*, which collectively form an *indifference map*. With the help of some further assumptions about their shape these maps have become the accepted basis for the economics of consumer behaviour.

In the 19th century it was thought that a definite measure of desirability could be constructed; a consumer would derive a given number of 'utils' from each package of goods, more the more desirable the combination. Thus, utility was measured on a *cardinal* basis with quantities, rather than the *ordinal* principle with just comparisons. In fact, it is usually sufficient only to rank preferences and the question of measurability has now been dropped.

An alternative framework has been proposed by J. von Neumann and O. Morgenstern who suggested a more meaningful comparison could be made by asking the consumer to make a choice between lotteries, e.g. between a 1 : 10 chance of winning a bottle of whisky, or a 1 : 1000 chance of a holiday in Bermuda. By adjusting the probabilities in the lotteries, the indifference surface could be traced. This removes any problems that otherwise occur with the division of goods into infinitesimally small units, and makes a more meaningful basis for comparisons. It is argued, though, that the element of risk distorts the actual judgements which would not usually be made in such sporting situations. This is perhaps a reflection of the difficulty of placing risk in any economic framework at all, rather than the suitability of the approach.

2.2 Basic Assumptions

Before examining the consumers' economic behaviour it is necessary to point to some basic assumptions about the form of the function f. This will later help spell out the basis for behaviour.

The consumer is assumed to be *rational*, i.e. the relationship that describes his indifference surface has two properties,

(*a*) for two packages A and B, either A is preferred to B, A and B are equally preferable, or B is preferred to A; and

(*b*) the evaluation is transitive, and so if A is preferred to B and B to C, then A is preferred to C. Transitivity has the same implication when just one of the pairs A, B or B, C are equally preferable. If A is equally preferable to B, however, and B likewise to C, then A is equally preferable to C. The properties help to ensure that the indifference surfaces do not intersect and that the evaluations are consistent with each other.

In anticipation of what follows, it is useful at this stage to make a further assumption,

(*c*) that the indifference surfaces are continuous, without any holes. It is sufficient, when package A is at least as desirable as B, which in turn is at least as desirable as C, for there to exist a package D which is as desirable as B and yet is made up of quantities x_{Dj}, $x_{Dj} = sx_{Aj} + (1-s)x_{Cj}$ where x_{Aj} and x_{Cj} are quantities of goods X_j in the packages A and C respectively and s is a suitably chosen value, $0 \leqslant s \leqslant 1$. Altogether this is a somewhat unreal situation because it assumes that quantities of all goods can be subjected to very small changes. It is obviously reasonable in some cases, e.g. meat and cheese, and yet not in others, e.g. cars and gramophone records.

It has become customary to add an observation about human behaviour to place a further restriction on the shape of the indifference surfaces. This concerns what is usually called the *marginal rate of*

Consumer Behaviour

substitution, the rate of trade-off between goods along the indifference curves as the quantity combinations are varied. The point is that goods generally become less attractive as their quantity is increased and, as economists first thought, the amount of utility gained in cardinal terms by a unit increase in a good decreases as the quantity of that good increases. This has been referred to as *the law of diminishing marginal utility*. In the case of ordinal utility it can be illustrated

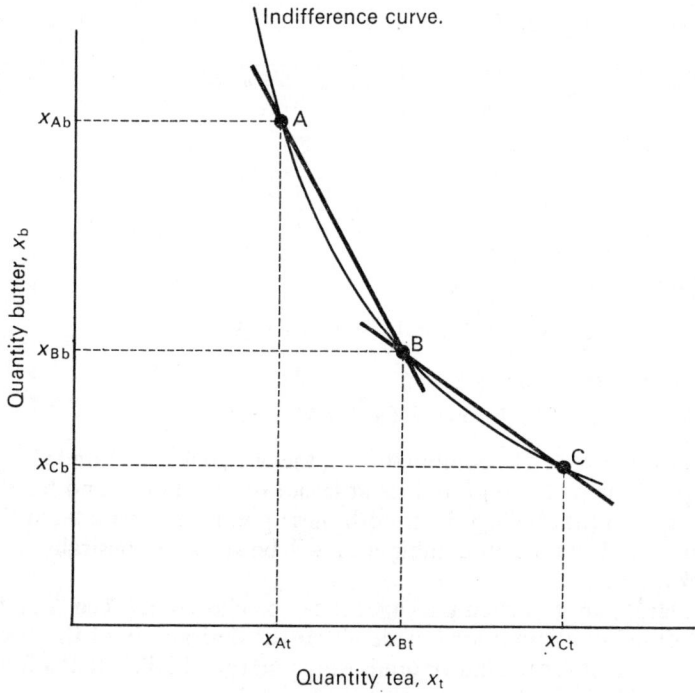

Fig. 2.1 Three combinations of tea and butter between which the consumer is indifferent.

by considering again the earlier example of packages containing different quantities of tea and butter. In particular, consider three packages A, B and C between which the consumer is indifferent and also which display the required property. In Fig. 2.1 the three combinations are marked out along the two axes representing quantities x_t of tea and x_b of butter. Looking at package B, it is possible to make a trade-off of tea against butter and move to either point A or C. In terms of quantities of tea and butter the two trade-off rates are

$$\frac{x_{Ab} - x_{Bb}}{x_{Bt} - x_{At}} \text{ and } \frac{x_{Bb} - x_{Cb}}{x_{Ct} - x_{Bt}} \text{ respectively.}$$

What the law of diminishing marginal returns infers is that, while the quantity of tea increases and both goods are still desirable, this trade-off decreases, i.e. (A5)

$$\frac{x_{Ab} - x_{Bb}}{x_{Bt} - x_{At}} \geqslant \frac{x_{Bb} - x_{Cb}}{x_{Ct} - x_{Bt}}$$

and so, for some positive values r,

$$\frac{x_{Ab} - x_{Bb}}{x_{Bb} - x_{Cb}} \geqslant r \geqslant \frac{x_{Bt} - x_{At}}{x_{Ct} - x_{Bt}}$$

By choosing a value

$$s = \frac{1}{1 + r},$$

this gives both

$$s\,x_{Ab} + (1 - s)x_{Cb} \geqslant x_{Bb}$$

and

$$s\,x_{At} + (1 - s)x_{Ct} \geqslant x_{Bt}$$

where $0 \leqslant s \leqslant 1$. The combination of the two packages A and C in the proportions $s:(1 - s)$ provides at least as much butter and tea as is included in the package B. If both these goods are desirable in their own right then the new combination will be at least as desirable as the package B.

A large range of such packages B can be chosen between A and C, and different assumptions made about the desirability of the goods. It is sufficient for the law of diminishing marginal utility that a fourth assumption is made,

(d) the utility function f is concave (A6), and so a consumer who is indifferent between two packages A and C will either be indifferent to or prefer a new package B constructed from a combination of the other two sets of quantities, namely

$$x_{Bj} = sx_{Aj} + (1 - s)x_{Cj},\ 0 \leqslant s \leqslant 1, j = 1\ldots n.$$

Altogether, the assumptions allow the indifference surfaces to be drawn like contours on a map. In Fig. 2.2 three possible shapes are illustrated in terms of trade-offs between two goods A and B. Points within the positive quadrants describe the various combinations and the four curves a, b, c and d indicate increasing levels of satisfaction.

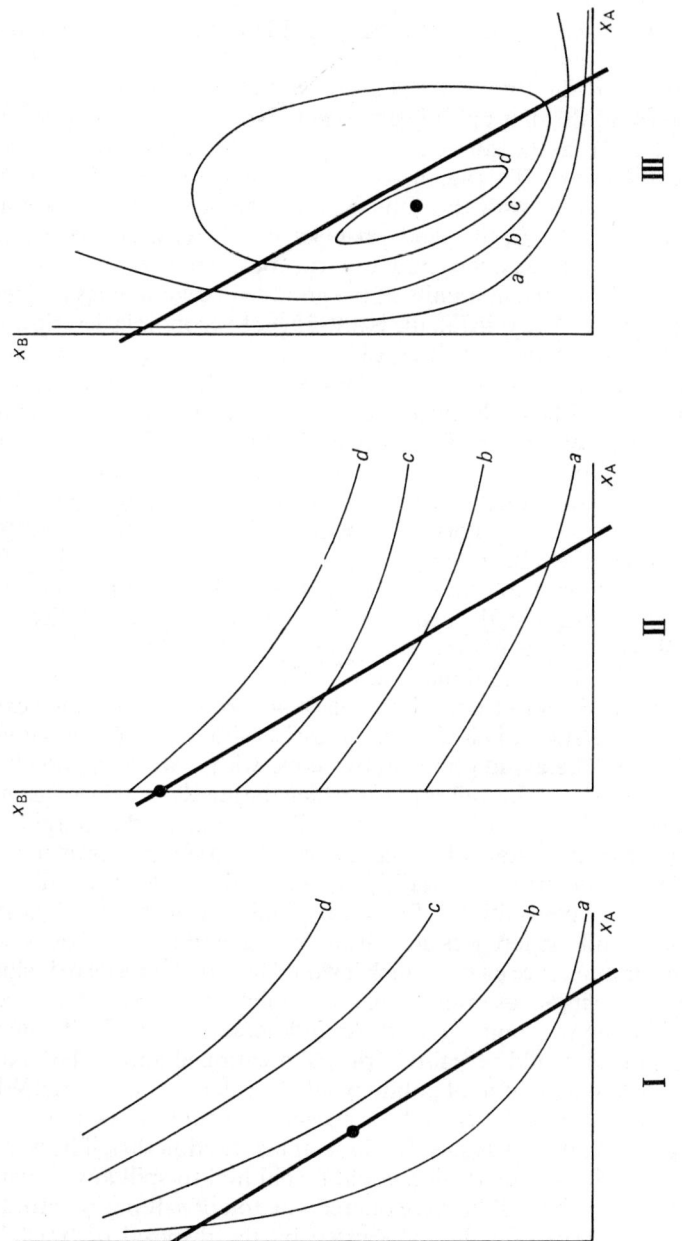

Fig. 2.2 Three possible shapes for the indifference map

Of the three shapes, the first (in Fig. 2.2.I) is the most common in economic discussions. The curves are convex to the origin (A9) and asymptotic to the two axes. This shows that the goods are always desirable and the first unit of each good is irreplaceable. The second (in Fig. 2.2.II) has the same convex shapes but this time they are allowed to meet the x_B axis. This again occurs in economic discussions but less frequently. Along with the similar situations where the curves are asymptotic to the x_B axis and yet meet the x_A axis, and where the curves meet both axes, the goods are still considered desirable but it is now possible for the first units of the goods to be sometimes replaced by other goods. The third shape is a stranger to economic descriptions and allows the consumer to consider points where an increase in at least one of the goods A and B is undesirable. This is a generalization that naturally follows the introduction of mathematical programming through the assumption of concave utility functions. The indifference curves turn round on themselves as the satisfaction falls away. If Fig. 2.2 is thought of as showing the slopes of mountains which increase in height in a north-easterly direction from the origin, then the third case as illustrated contains the 'peak' within the diagram. Both goods then stop being desirable. Alternatively, if only one good becomes undesirable, the map would contain a 'ridge' which rises in a general northerly or easterly direction.

Economics has traditionally always thought of goods as desirable and the extension to cases where this is not true deserves some extra comment. Firstly, it is just an extension to situations not previously considered. The assumptions above cope with a world in which all goods are desirable as well as one in which the goods that the consumer includes in his comparisons are not all desirable at the margin. Although they may not all be necessary, the assumptions made are sufficient to describe the traditional economic world. Secondly, the pressures and conventions of modern life distort the 'natural' pattern of tastes and preferences and lead to a possibility of backward-bending indifference curves which it would be more realistic to include. Take, for a simple example, table salt which, by convention, is consumed in one way only, in food. An indifference map of salt against, say, potatoes would reveal the 'ridges' mentioned above. Too much or too little salt per unit of potato would be equally undesirable. What the consumer would like to do is accept the situation with more salt and throw away the surplus. But look at his reaction then if he were at all superstitious! Convention could forbid him to spill any. Equally, look at his problem if he were offered one ton of salt per potato. In a world conscious of pollution caused by the disposal of 'waste', it need not necessarily be a simple matter to remove the surplus.

The indifference curves, whether the goods are desirable or not, lead to an explanation of how a consumer alters his pattern of expenditure in the face of changes in prices of the goods. This involves a relationship described usually by the *demand curves*. These are a set of curves drawn to illustrate how the quantities purchased of particular goods vary as their prices change. Each curve, with quantity on one axis and price on the other, relates to one good only and, while the price of that good changes, the prices of all other goods remain the same. The derivation of a demand curve will be shown first by means of an example and then extended to the general situation.

2.3 A Two-Good Example

Start by considering that a consumer spends his income Y on just two goods A and B. He buys them in quantities x_A and x_B at prices p_A and p_B. It is assumed that the consumer lives in a very simple world and distributes his earned income either by purchasing goods within a period of time, or alternatively throwing his money away. There is no notion of saving by purchasing capital goods. (This is introduced in chapter 10.) Therefore, as the only restriction is that he can spend no more than his income, but possibly less, it can be said of his expenditure that

$$p_A x_A + p_B x_B \leqslant Y$$

If he reached a point where he exhausted his income, the trade-off between goods at the limit would be the ratio p_A/p_B, a constant. It is possible to trace all such combinations on a diagram with the quantities x_A and x_B along the axes. They would lie along the straight lines drawn in each of the figures in Fig. 2.2. Each line cuts off a triangular convex region bounded by itself and the two axes (A8, A10). Any combination of goods within this triangle satisfies the income constraint and is therefore called *feasible*.

It is now possible to build up a behaviour pattern. The consumer would be expected to choose from within the triangle of feasibility the point that gives him the greatest satisfaction, the 'highest' point judged from the pattern of contours. In the three cases of Fig. 2.2 this will lead to different combinations of quantities of the two goods. In the first case the 'best' combination will be at a point on the income constraint which just touches some contour between the curves *a* and *b*. Both goods will be included. In the second case the indifference curves are flatter than the budget line and most satisfaction will be derived by spending all the income on good B, i.e. $x_A = 0$, $x_B = Y/p_B$. Finally, in the third case the 'best' combination will be found at the 'peak' of the mountain. This is inside the triangle of feasibility and not all the income will be spent.

To help formalize the above procedure assume that the partial derivatives exist for the function f with respect to the quantities x_A and x_B (A12). The slope of the indifference contour in the diagrams is then given by the ratio

$$-\frac{\delta f}{\delta x_A}\bigg/\frac{\delta f}{\delta x_B}$$

and the three cases can be classified as follows:

I. Both goods are desirable, i.e.

$$\frac{\delta f}{\delta x_A}, \frac{\delta f}{\delta x_B} > 0,$$

at all points inside the feasible region and a pair of values for the variables x_A and x_B can be found such that

$$\frac{\delta f}{\delta x_A} p_B - \frac{\delta f}{\delta x_B} p_A = 0$$

The solution to this equation indicates the position of the optimum. Then the slope of the income constraint is equal to that of the appropriate indifference curve.

II. Both goods are desirable, i.e.

$$\frac{\delta f}{\delta x_A}, \frac{\delta f}{\delta x_B} > 0$$

and no solution exists to the equation of slopes. In fact,

$$\frac{\delta f}{\delta x_A} p_B - \frac{\delta f}{\delta x_B} p_A < 0$$

for all points within the region. The optimal utility is found at the point

$$(x_A, x_B) = \left(0, \frac{Y}{p_B}\right)$$

III. For some pair of quantities (x_A^0, x_B^0) inside the feasible region

$$\frac{\delta f}{\delta x_A} = \frac{\delta f}{\delta x_B} = 0$$

The point of greatest utility will be $(x_A, x_B) = (x_A^0, x_B^0)$.

The above description outlines precisely the important properties of the optima in the earlier diagrams of Fig. 2.2 and shows how the 'best' combination of goods can be evaluated. Therefore it indicates how a quantity–price combination represented by a point on the

Consumer Behaviour

demand curve can be derived. More can be said about small moves along the demand curve that result from changes in price, however, and a further look at the two-good example points to the resulting effects on quantity.

If a small price change is made at the optimum, the above conditions will still hold and the connection between price changes dp_A and dp_B, and quantity changes dx_A and dx_B can be studied by considering again the three situations:

I. For the first case it is customary to look at the effects of price changes in two parts. Firstly, instead of making changes as might be expected, with all but prices kept constant, some adjustments are made simultaneously to income. While prices are changed, income is adjusted externally to maintain the level of satisfaction. So, if there is a price increase dp_A, dp_B (A11, A12), the changes in quantities can be written

$$df = \frac{\delta f}{\delta x_A} dx_A + \frac{\delta f}{\delta x_B} dx_B = 0$$

Because this represents a move along the indifference contour, the effect on the quantities is known as the *substitution effect*. In addition, the total differential of income can be expanded, so

$$dY = x_A dp_A + x_B dp_B + p_A dx_A + p_B dx_B$$
$$= x_A dp_A + x_B dp_B + p_A \left(\frac{\delta f}{\delta x_A} dx_A + \frac{\delta f}{\delta x_B} dx_B \right) \bigg/ \frac{\delta f}{\delta x_A}$$

because, at the optimum, the ratio of prices p_A and p_B equals that of partial derivatives

$$\frac{\delta f}{\delta x_A} \text{ and } \frac{\delta f}{\delta x_B}.$$

Therefore the increase in income required to keep satisfaction constant will be

$$dY = x_A dp_A + x_B dp_B$$

and provides an expression, in money terms, for the value of the price changes to the customer.

The second part requires a move back to the position which would be reached if instead income were kept constant. For the demand relationships there will be no compensating change in income, and the above substitution effect will have to be modified. This is done by means of the *income effect* which reflects a change in income while prices are kept constant. So a change along the demand curve can be built up from a total of a substitution effect plus an income effect in which the original income level is restored.

To look more closely at substitution, consider the effect of changing all the prices and quantities in the equation of line slopes. Taking the total differential of both sides provides (A12)

$$\frac{\delta^2 f}{\delta x_A^2} p_B \mathrm{d}x_A + \frac{\delta^2 f}{\delta x_A \delta x_B} p_B \mathrm{d}x_B + \frac{\delta f}{\delta x_A} \mathrm{d}p_B - \frac{\delta^2 f}{\delta x_A \delta x_B} p_A \mathrm{d}x_A$$

$$- \frac{\delta^2 f}{\delta x_B^2} p_A \mathrm{d}x_B - \frac{\delta f}{\delta x_B} \mathrm{d}p_A = 0$$

Multiplying through by $\mathrm{d}x_A$ gives, bearing in mind that total satisfaction is held constant and so $p_A \mathrm{d}x_A + p_B \mathrm{d}x_B = 0$,

$$p_B \left(\frac{\delta^2 f}{\delta x_A^2} \mathrm{d}x_A^2 + 2 \frac{\delta^2 f}{\delta x_A \delta x_B} \mathrm{d}x_A \mathrm{d}x_B + \frac{\delta^2 f}{\delta x_B^2} \mathrm{d}x_B^2 \right)$$

$$+ \frac{\delta f}{\delta x_A} \mathrm{d}p_B \mathrm{d}x_A - \frac{\delta f}{\delta x_B} \mathrm{d}p_A \mathrm{d}x_A = 0$$

Because the function f is concave, the first term is less than or equal to zero (A13), and so

$$\left(\frac{\delta f}{\delta x_A} \mathrm{d}p_B - \frac{\delta f}{\delta x_B} \mathrm{d}p_A \right) \mathrm{d}x_A \geqslant 0$$

By a similar argument,

$$\left(\frac{\delta f}{\delta x_A} \mathrm{d}p_B - \frac{\delta f}{\delta x_B} \mathrm{d}p_A \right) \mathrm{d}x_B \leqslant 0$$

These two inequalities are useful for examining what happens in two particular situations:

(i) If $\mathrm{d}p_B = 0$, then $-\mathrm{d}p_A \mathrm{d}x_A \geqslant 0$ and $-\mathrm{d}p_A \mathrm{d}x_B \leqslant 0$

and

(ii) If $\mathrm{d}p_A = 0$, then $\mathrm{d}p_B \mathrm{d}x_A \geqslant 0$ and $\mathrm{d}p_B \mathrm{d}x_B \leqslant 0$.

This illustrates an important feature of the substitution effect, an increase in price of one good alone leads to a decrease in quantity of that good and an increase of the other. Even though there is a compensating change in income, there is still a substitution away from the good with the price rise.

The income effect that results from changing income back to its original value is not so predictable. There is no reason why it should reinforce or counteract any movement in the substitution effect. With very few exceptions, though, it is reasonable to assume that the effect on quantities of goods will be close enough to a proportional one for the direction of the main changes to follow the substitution. As a result, if 'demand functions' are denoted by functions g^A and g^B which relate the quantities consumed of each good to all the prices, i.e. (A5)

$$x_A \equiv g^A(p_A, p_B) \text{ and } x_B \equiv g^B(p_A, p_B),$$

then the associated demand curves will usually be downward-sloping with respect to the same good, i.e.

$$\frac{\delta g^A}{\delta p_A} \leqslant 0 \text{ and } \frac{\delta g^B}{\delta p_B} \leqslant 0$$

So, while substitution round the indifference contour shifts the quantities away from the good with the price increase, the buying power of the original income is reduced, usually causing a further drop in quantity of that good bought.

II. For the second case, the solution is given by the two equations $x_A = 0$ and $x_B = Y/p_B$. There will be no change resulting from a small variation in the price of good A. On the other hand, for good B, a price increase will reduce the quantity purchased still leaving a zero quantity for good A. The total effect will be to reduce satisfaction through an income effect. The substitution effect will be zero.

III. For the third case, the actual solution is independent of the budget constraint for small changes in prices. There will be no substitution or income effects and no change in total satisfaction.

2.4 A General Model of Demand

For the example there were only two goods consumed and consideration was given to just three sets of indifference curves. In the general case, there will be a larger number of goods and curve shapes, and it is of interest to know whether the arguments used above still hold. The broad answer to this is 'yes', and reassurance of this statement is given by a set of mathematical statements known as the Kuhn–Tucker conditions. They show that, in the situation of many goods, the classification of Fig. 2.2 is sufficient to describe all the types of optimal combinations of goods that could occur.

The Kuhn–Tucker conditions have arisen, not through economics, but through mathematical programming. They are a set of properties of an optimal point that lies inside a convex region and is judged on the basis of a concave function (A3, A8). The full statement of the conditions appears complicated and is given in Appendix B. It can be interpreted by thinking of points in either two-, three- or even n-dimensional space each leading to a value of the function (A2).

An example is where points on a map indicate heights on a 'well-rounded' hill (A2, A6). If an optimum is sought while these points are constrained inside a convex region (A3, A8), e.g. contained within a field on the side of the hill, then, either the best point lies well inside the region, or it lies on the boundary and is stopped from moving further by the constraints. The Kuhn–Tucker conditions spell out these two possibilities in general terms and, in the latter case, point out that, at an optimum, the direction in which a move could best be made, the preferred direction, will not make an acute angle with the boundary of the convex region. For the example of the field on the side of the hill, if the highest point lies on the edge of the field, the line of steepest ascent will make a non-acute angle with the edges as they would be marked on a map. This possibility is illustrated in Fig. 2.3.

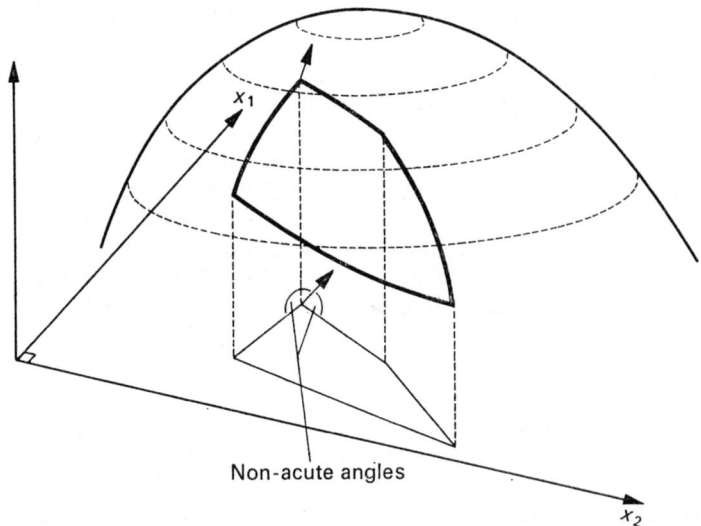

Fig. 2.3 The highest point within a field on the side of a well-rounded hill.

The complexity of the statement of the conditions seems quite remote from the line of steepest ascent and its non-acute angle with the edge of the field. Nevertheless the example of the field is not that different to the feasible region for the two-good example of consumer behaviour for which the nature of the optima has been explored. Therefore by applying the conditions to the general case of consumer demand a link can be maintained with the simple interpretation and yet a useful insight can be gained both into the economics of consumer demand and the mathematics of the Kuhn–Tucker conditions.

Consumer Behaviour

For our immediate purpose the conditions will be specifically used to describe the properties of the optimal combination of quantities of goods $(x_1^0, x_2^0, \ldots x_n^0)$ that provide the greatest satisfaction as defined by the concave function $f(x_1, x_2, \ldots x_n)$. The variables are subjected to the budget constraint

$$\sum_{j=1}^{n} p_j x_j - Y \leqslant 0 \qquad (A5)$$

where prices p_j are all non-negative and, because they represent quantities consumed,

$$x_j \geqslant 0, j = 1 \ldots n$$

As the linear expression in the budget constraint is a convex function, the Kuhn–Tucker conditions can be applied. They state that a non-negative value y^0 can be found such that

$$-\frac{\delta f}{\delta x_j} + y^0 p_j \geqslant 0, j = 1 \ldots n$$

$$\sum_{j=1}^{n} \left(-\frac{\delta f}{\delta x_j} + y^0 p_j \right) x_j^0 = 0$$

and

$$\left(\sum_{j=1}^{n} p_j x_j - Y \right) y^0 = 0$$

Moreover, it is only at the optimum that such a value can be found.

So that a parallel can be drawn with the example of the last section, consider the value of the expression

$$\left(\frac{\delta f}{\delta x_A} p_B - \frac{\delta f}{\delta x_B} p_A \right)$$

at the optimum where A and B are two goods chosen from all the goods. If it is forced to be negative at all points in the feasible region, then, in order to satisfy the second condition

$$\left(-\frac{\delta f}{\delta x_B} + y^0 p_B \right) x_B^0 = 0$$

and it must follow that

$$\frac{p_B}{p_A} \left(-\frac{\delta f}{\delta x_A} + y^0 p_A \right) > -\frac{\delta f}{\delta x_B} + y^0 p_B = 0$$

Hence either x_A^0 or $x_B^0 = 0$. Similarly, if it is forced to be positive within the region, either x_B^0 or $x_A^0 = 0$. Thus, in the general situation, if the slopes of the indifference surface and the budget hyperplane (A10) are not equal, the optimal solution lies on one of the axes.

Further classification of the positions of the optima can be derived from the partial derivatives. If, for all points in the feasible region, at least one partial derivative is positive, then, so that the condition

$$-\frac{\delta f}{\delta x_j} + y^0 p_j \geqslant 0$$

can hold $y^0 p_j > 0$ and it follows that $y^0 > 0$. Therefore, to uphold the last equation in the conditions,

$$\sum_{j=1}^{n} p_j x_j - Y = 0$$

i.e. the optimum lies on the budget constraint. Otherwise, for some point all the partial derivations are zero and a choice of a zero value of y will satisfy the Kuhn–Tucker conditions. This point will be an optimum. Hence, depending first on the relationship between the slopes of the indifference surface and budget constraint, and now on the value of the partial derivatives, the parallels to cases I, II and III are drawn. The previous classification is sufficiently broad to cover the generalization to many goods.

One important difference is the introduction of the variable y and it is worth attempting to interpret the value it takes. When it is positive in the solution, the optimum lies on the budget constraint. If this constraint were relaxed by increasing income Y, an overall higher level of satisfaction could be obtained by increasing quantities of the goods already held in positive quantities up to the new position of the constraint. Denoting increases by df, dY and dx, the change can be evaluated from the two equations

$$df = \sum_j \frac{\delta f}{\delta x_j} dx_j^0$$

$$dY = \sum_j p_j dx_j^0$$

where the summations include only indices j for those goods for which $x_j > 0$. So that the second condition can be upheld in the Kuhn–Tucker statement, it must also be true for these goods that

$$-\frac{\delta f}{\delta x_j} + y^0 p_j = 0$$

Substituting for the partial derivatives, the above equations give

$$df = \sum_j p_j y^0 dx_j^0 = y^0 dY$$

Consumer Behaviour

and the value y^0 indicates the effect on total satisfaction of a money increase in spending power. This, in the jargon of cardinal economics, is called the *marginal utility of income*. It provides a quantitative view of the income effect.

The reappearance of the income effect brings back the question of effects of changes discussed in the simpler case. The substitution effects and expectation of a downward sloping demand curve carry over, and can be deduced by the direct extension of previous arguments. This relies on the examination of arrays of derivatives and requires a considerable amount of manipulation. It will not be pursued here.

2.5 A Generalized Model of Consumer Behaviour

The behaviour model that has been discussed so far has been based on the principle of maximizing satisfaction subject to the fixed budget constraint. This is an approach adopted in modern economics where the consumer is expected to be sufficiently well paid to be able to exercise choice in his expenditure. In early economic theory the emphasis was quite different, with the consumer leading a peasant's subsistence existence. The decisions that concerned him were simple, how to best satisfy the basic requirements of life.

There is a well-known programming problem that looks at the question of subsistence with regard to the level of nutrients required in a diet. Suppose that a daily diet is represented by the quantities x_j of foods $X_j, j = 1 \ldots n$. Its suitability for a particular 'consumer' can be judged by its satisfying certain requirements with regard to the nutrients provided. For example, the total protein value would be expected to reach at least some minimum level, as would the calorific value and the iron content. So it might be said that

$$f_i(x_1, x_2, \ldots x_n) \geqslant L_i, i = 1 \ldots m$$

where f_i are the mechanisms for computing the total amount of nutrients N_i and L_i are the lower subsistence limits. The problem hinges on the appropriate choice of quantities for the diet so that expenditure on food is at a minimum. If the prices of foods X_j are p_j, this will be a matter of minimizing the total cost $\sum_{j=1}^{n} p_j x_j$. Whereas in the last section the assessment of the quantities x_j by the consumer was made by the utility function f which was maximized, it is now made in the constraint functions f_i. Also, the expression for total cost which was previously in the constraint is now to be minimized.

The nutrition problem is significant in that it represents a complete reversal of the previous demand model. The approach has been developed considerably in the fields of fuel-blending and livestock feeding.

From the point of view of the consumer it emphasizes that a full formulation of behaviour might be expected to include maintenance of standards as well as maximization of satisfaction.

A generalized behaviour model can now be formulated on the basis of the nutrition problem. Suppose that expenditure by a complete household on goods $X_j, j = 1 \ldots n$, is based on a set of general standards of the type described above. These can be thought of as reflecting the 'style of life' of the consumer and his family. Examples are the need to make commuting, school and shopping journeys, the wish to maintain a specific standard of housing, or the requirements of car ownership. The standards are described by the inequalities

$$L_i - f_i(x_1, x_2, \ldots x_n) \leqslant 0, i = 1 \ldots m,$$

where now f_i are concave functions of the non-negative quantities x_j, and L_i are constants.

The expenditure on goods X_j can be judged not only in terms of money, but also in terms of other media of exchange. A popular example is the commodity time. The overall aim, therefore, will be to minimize some generalized expenditure function made up from a weighted combination of the expenditure in each medium. This can be written as

$$\sum_{k=1}^{p} y_k^0 g_k(x_1, x_2, \ldots x_n)$$

where g_k are convex functions, $k = 1 \ldots p$, representing the cost in terms of exchange medium k of the selection of goods $x_1, \ldots x_n$. The set of non-negative coefficients y_k^0 are the relative weighting of the media against each other. For example, they might indicate the 'value' of time, or the relative importance of the time of different members of the household.

If the Kuhn–Tucker conditions are translated in terms of the above optimization problem, the minimum expenditure pattern $(x_1^0, x_2^0, \ldots x_n^0)$ will be associated with a particular set of non-negative values which satisfy the conditions. Denote these by $z_i^0, i = 1 \ldots m$. Just as the value y^0 indicated the effect of changes in the income constraint in the last section, the values z_i^0 now give the effect of changes in the constraint constants L_i. Thus they express the relative importance of the different standards as they are balanced against each other in the optimal solution.

What is interesting is that these values z_i^0 can be used to formulate an equivalent maximization problem. It will involve the maximization of a utility function $\sum_{i=1}^{m} z_i^0 f_i(x_1, x_2, \ldots x_n)$ made up by a weighted sum of the same criteria as were used in the statement of standards.

Consumer Behaviour

The optimization is subjected to 'budget' constraints

$$g_k(x_1, x_2, \ldots x_n) \leqslant M_k, k = 1 \ldots p$$

i.e.

$$g_k(x_1, x_2, \ldots x_n) - M_k \leqslant 0, k = 1 \ldots p$$

where the constants M_k are values of the functions g_k evaluated at the optimal point in the minimization problem. A new set of Kuhn-Tucker conditions can be derived, this time for the maximization problem. These conditions involve another set of values which can be denoted by y_k^0 and so contain the same expressions as they did for the minimization problem. In both cases it is required that

$$\sum_{k=1}^{p} y_k^0 \frac{\delta g_k}{\delta x_j} - \sum_{i=1}^{m} z_i^0 \frac{\delta f_i}{\delta x_j} \geqslant 0, j = 1 \ldots n$$

and

$$\sum_{j=1}^{n} \left(\sum_{k=1}^{p} y_k^0 \frac{\delta g_k}{\delta x_j} - \sum_{i=1}^{m} z_i^0 \frac{\delta f_i}{\delta x_j} \right) x_j^0 = 0$$

The similarity of the two sets of conditions can be exploited. Because of the way the constants M_k are constructed, the sets of values y_k^0 and x_j^0 used in the minimization problem will satisfy all the maximization conditions, namely the two above and

$$\sum_{k=1}^{p} (g_k(x_1, x_2, \ldots x_n) - M_k) y_k^0 = 0$$

Therefore, given an original set of weights y_k^0, a solution might be found to the minimization problem for the quantities x_j^0. A corresponding maximization problem can be constructed by a suitable choice of weights z_i^0 and constants M_k, and has the same solution. Moreover, if the original minimization problem is modified so that the constraint constants L_i are set equal to the values of functions f_i evaluated at the new optimum, then while the solution x_j^0 is not changed, the relationship of the maximization to the minimization problem becomes the same as that of the minimization to the maximization problem.

The relationship between the two problems raises an interesting point. Any expenditure pattern $(x_1, x_2, \ldots x_n)$ can be interpreted as either a maximization of utility or a minimization of cost. Both approaches involve valuations in the form of relative weightings. These same valuations are now playing a large part in the judgement of government projects from a social standpoint and it is useful to know that they can be placed in an economic framework. The question that should immediately follow though, is more difficult and will be set to one side. It asks how they might be measured.

2.6 A Time Allocation Model

A natural development of consumer theory would seem to be the behaviour of individuals when they have enough time available to organize activities according to their personal wishes. Just as choice was introduced into expenditure patterns now it is the turn for freedom in programming time. Some indications of moves in this direction have already been the assessment of benefits derived from building the M1 motorway and the London Underground Victoria line, as well as the siting of the Third London Airport. In these cases travellers would be expected to re-schedule their activities as a result of changes in journey time. The question for the planners is how these time changes can be valued or, in other words, what weighting can be applied to time relative to money.

To establish a model, broaden the principles of demand to assume that a consumer derives satisfaction from the programme of activities $A_i, i = 1 \ldots m$ that he follows through a given time period, say a day. Each activity A_i starts at a time t_i and ends at time t_{i+1} when the next activity, A_{i+1}, begins. It also involves the consumption of goods $X_j, j = 1 \ldots n$ in quantities x_{ij}. Suppose that it is possible to derive a measure f of total satisfaction from a detailed description of the day's events

$$f \equiv f(t_i, x_{ij}; i = 1 \ldots m, j = 1 \ldots n)$$

It would be expected that the consumer would attempt to maximize satisfaction subject to whatever constraints might be imposed.

The list of possible constraints starts with the consumer's budget. If Y denotes disposable income and $p_j, j = 1 \ldots n$, the prices of goods X_j, then the income constraint would be

$$\sum_{i=1}^{m} \sum_{j=1}^{n} p_j x_{ij} - Y \leqslant 0$$

There will also be basic time constraints

$$t_1 = 0$$

$$t_{m+1} = T$$

where 0 and T are the time markers for the beginning and end of the day. Another condition is that

$$t_{i+1} \geqslant t_i, i = 1 \ldots m$$

which indicates that one activity cannot start before the previous one has finished. Less obvious is the point that a number of times will be fixed for the consumer, e.g. the start and finish times for work, and also some time intervals will be fixed in length, e.g. journey times. As a result more constraints can be added to the list, e.g.

$$t_{s-1} = t_s^0 - \tau_{s-1}^0$$
$$t_s = t_s^0$$

where the $(s-1)$th activity is the journey to work, the sth activity work itself, t_s^0 the work start time and τ_{s-1}^0 the length of the work journey. These two examples state that the journey-to-work and work activities must start at given times.

To bring the problem into line with the framework of earlier sections define a new variable $\tau_i \equiv t_{i+1} - t_i$ to take over the description of the daily programme. The problem can then be stated in a more familiar form using a new function g for satisfaction.

Maximize $g(\tau_i, x_{ij}; i = 1 \ldots m, j = 1 \ldots n)$
subject to

$$\sum_{i=1}^{m} \sum_{j=1}^{n} p_j x_{ij} - Y \leqslant 0$$

$$\tau_{s-1} = \tau_{s-1}^0$$

$$\sum_{i=1}^{s-2} \tau_i = t_s^0 - \tau_{s-1}^0$$

$$\sum_{i=s}^{m} \tau_i = T - t_s^0$$

and

$$\tau_i, x_{ij} \geqslant 0, i = 1 \ldots m, j = 1 \ldots n$$

As the amount of time given up to an activity can be treated in a similar way to goods consumed, it is reasonable to expect the law of diminishing marginal utility to apply. The function g can therefore be considered concave in all the variables τ_i and x_{ij} that can still be adjusted by the consumer. (There is no need to require this property for the fixed journey time.) In fact the interpretation of the law of diminishing marginal utility can be broadened to include disutility. After all, time consumed in some activities beyond an initial period often provides a disutility which increases with time. An example is watching a 'bad' film at the cinema when a short or long stay would create curiosity or boredom respectively with less satisfaction and indifference curves of type III would be required to describe tastes and preferences.

Returning to the time allocation model for commuting to work, an application of the Kuhn–Tucker conditions provides a set of variables y_1, y_2 and y_3 for which

$$-\frac{\delta g}{\delta x_{ij}} + p_j y_1 = 0, i = 1 \ldots m, j = 1 \ldots n$$

$$-\frac{\delta g}{\delta \tau_i} + y_2 = 0, i = 1 \ldots s - 2$$

and

$$-\frac{\delta g}{\delta \tau_i} + y_3 = 0, i = s \ldots m$$

when the appropriate value of x_{ij} or τ_i is greater than zero. In short, there are values $y_1{}^0$, $y_2{}^0$, $y_3{}^0 \geqslant 0$ which represent the relative importance, and hence the effect on total satisfaction of relaxations, of the constraints, and it is therefore possible to determine the trade-off between money income and the time changes that might result from investment projects. In the model developed here, a cut in the journey time will be worth a change in income at the rate of $y_1{}^0/y_2{}^0$. Similarly, changes in work start-time that result from an effort to stagger the peak hour would be worth a money trade-off of $y_1{}^0/(y_3{}^0 - y_2{}^0)$.

This framework will be developed in chapter 7 to indicate the possible effect that congestion has on the distribution of peak-hour traffic flows in an urban area. For the moment, though, it demonstrates how consumer behaviour becomes more elaborate when a second medium of exchange, time, is added to the first, money.

3 Production Planning

Whereas the framework for consumer behaviour is built around the concepts of preference curves or standards of living, the basis for examining the behaviour of firms that eventually supply the consumer is much more clear cut. Broadly, there are two steps, the first involving the actual planning of production processes once the details such as production targets, buying price for components and selling price for the product have been set. This can be thought of as *short-term* planning where the scope for action is limited typically to decisions affecting the immediate future. The second step takes a look at the *long term* and involves broader issues of expansion or contraction of total production, price-setting and investment particularly with regard to capital equipment. The breakdown is convenient from the point of view of demarcation between jobs within the firm. The 'engineers' would be expected to cope with the detail of production management, taking short-term decisions about the internal workings of the firm, while the 'managing directors', or *entrepreneurs* as they have become known in economic jargon, take long-term decisions in the context of the external markets through which the firm operates.

In general terms, economics has traditionally helped foster these distinctions, and has considered the behaviour of firms as a summary of the way enterpreneurs respond to and control the prices of components —the *inputs* of the firm's production processes—and the prices of products, the *outputs*. Their action is studied through the quantities and prices of goods that are bought and sold, and no reference is made to the detail of the actual production management. From the entrepreneur's standpoint the firm is quite simply a 'black-box' in which, given a set of input quantities, a team of engineers will endeavour, somehow, to produce the greatest quantities of the outputs. The efforts of the engineers are summed up in a single relationship known as the *production function*, a formula that provides quantities output in terms of quantities input.

The introduction of mathematical programming has the effect of merging together the two functions of the engineer and managing director, and has the added advantage of bringing in an element of accounting. Altogether these are important moves for there results one framework within which the approaches can be fitted and hence a complete basis on which the overall behaviour of the firm can be discussed. The different emphasis is due to the subject not being aimed initially in the direction of economic theory. It has been developed as a tool for making decisions in terms of actual quantities in planning problems that face the management of particular firms at specific points in time. Therefore, in order to reach the general behaviour of the firm as an economic unit, it will be necessary to consider what advice might be given to firms faced with a number of production problems. This will be called *production planning* and takes up the present and next chapters. If it is then assumed that all entrepreneurs heed the advice in real situations, or at least behave as though they do, it will be possible to build up a general pattern of behaviour of the firm. In this wider sense they will be confronted by, and have to react to, consumers in situations pursued in chapter 5.

3.1 Meeting a Production Target

To begin with, consider an example where a firm has to organize its production to meet a fixed output target. It involves the assembly of components for the car industry for which a strict weekly consignment of 1000 casings is required. They are made by welding together pieces of metal that have been cut and pressed into shape. Suppose there are three different processes A, B and C differing through the technique of welding and the number of pieces cut for each casing. A problem arises about the split of production between the processes in the light of a number of restrictions on machinery available, floor space and manpower.

The eventual number of casings produced by each process can be denoted by the variables x_A, x_B and x_C. To be meaningful in terms of the problem they will have to be either zero or positive in value, i.e.

$$x_A, x_B, x_C \geqslant 0$$

For the output requirement to be met exactly,

$$x_A + x_B + x_C = 1000$$

Because this is an equality it will be possible to identify a final solution by just the two quantities x_A and x_B, the number of casings passing through process C making up the quota. Therefore, for simplicity, it will be taken that

$$x_C = 1000 - x_A - x_B \geqslant 0$$

Consider, in addition, that process A is slower than processes B or C because of the need to cut and weld more pieces. On the other hand,

Production Planning

process B is slower than process C because of different methods of welding. As a result, the respective production rates with the machinery available are, say, 500, 700 and 900 casings per week. Therefore, in terms of the production deadline, there will be three constraints

$$x_A \leqslant 500$$
$$x_B \leqslant 700$$
$$x_C = 1000 - x_A - x_B \leqslant 900$$

Suppose, finally, that the machinery for the three processes takes up different amounts of the 9600 sq. ft floor space. The rate of use of floor area is 5, 10 and 16 sq. ft to maintain a one casing per week output level on each of the processes A, B and C respectively. Therefore, a constraint on floor area is required,

$$5x_A + 10x_B + 16x_C \leqslant 9600$$

which, on substituting for x_C becomes

$$-11x_A - 6x_B \leqslant -6400$$

The problem has been reduced to a set of inequalities in which a number of restrictions are placed on the values of the quantities x_A and x_B. The effect of the constraints can be demonstrated by a diagram, Fig. 3.1, in which points represent the possible combinations of values. All the constraints are linear and the corresponding lines are plotted to indicate the combinations of values that meet exactly the limitations. If, then, the values are to obey the inequalities, the points considered must stay on one particular side of each of the lines. The only ones that do this for all the constraints simultaneously are those inside the shaded area *abcd*. This will be called the *feasible region* and represents the full range of possible solutions to the overall planning problem. The question remains of which particular point gives the 'best' combination of processes.

To define precisely what is meant by 'best', consider that the aim in this case is to cut to a minimum the cost of labour employed in the workshop. If the fixed total labour force were equally productive on all the processes but a bonus payment was required for process A, then an objective might be to pay the least number of bonuses, i.e. to minimize x_A. This will become the *objective function* for the problem and the optimal situation will be achieved when process A works at the lowest possible level, at point *c* in the diagram. This point lies on the intersection of the two lines *dc* and *bc* whose equations are

$$-11x_A - 6x_B = -6400$$

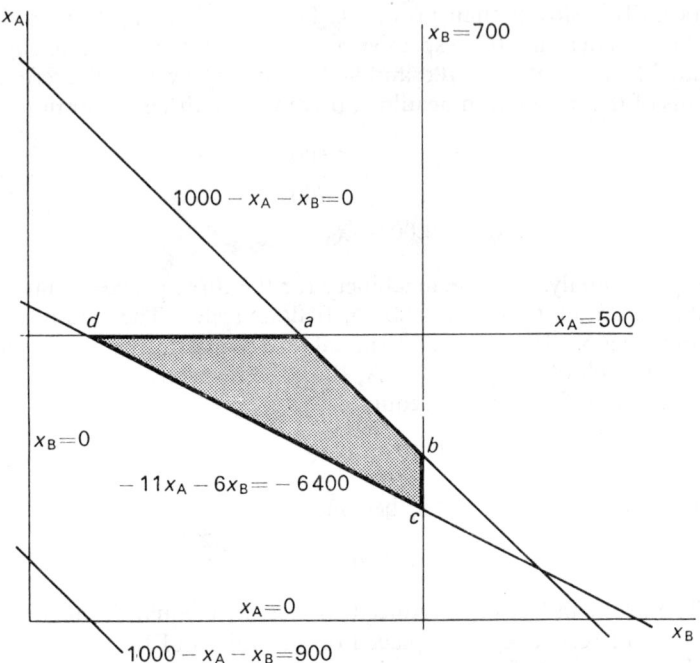

Fig. 3.1 Representation of constraints on the number of casings.

and

$$x_B = 700$$

Solving the equations gives $x_A = 200$, $x_B = 700$ and, by recalling the earlier elimination of x_C, $x_C = 1000 - x_A - x_B = 100$. All the other constraints are satisfied by strict inequalities,

$$1000 - x_A - x_B = 100 < 900$$
$$x_A = 200 < 500$$
$$x = 1000 - x_A - x_B = 100 > 0$$

and

$$x_A, x_B > 0$$

Similarly, if the bonus had applied to process B only, the optimal solution would be indicated by point *d*, which is furthest in the direction of decreasing quantity x_B. The solution could then be found by solving the equations

$$x_A = 500$$

Production Planning

and

$$-11x_A - 6x_B = -6400$$

i.e. $x_A = 500$, $x_B = 150$ and $x_C = 1000 - x_A - x_B = 350$.

What, though, if the bonus had applied equally to processes A and B? It would then be required to minimize the sum $(x_A + x_B)$ which means looking in the direction where both variables x_A and x_B are decreasing together. This will involve moving through the area *abcd* at right angles to the contours denoting constant sum $(x_A + x_B)$ and shown in Fig. 3.2 superimposed on the feasible region. The corner *d*

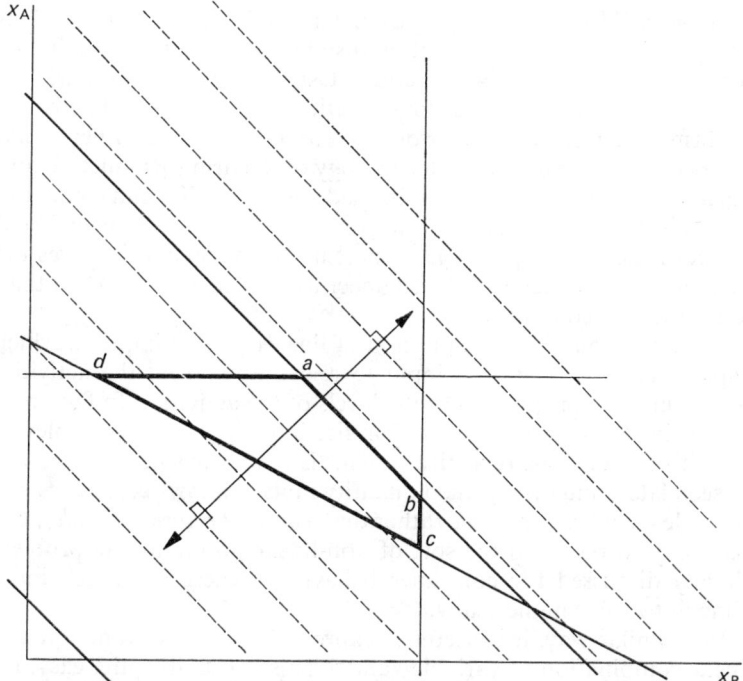

Fig. 3.2 Contours of constant sum $(x_A + x_B)$ superimposed on the feasible region.

will again be pinpointed to give $x_A = 500$, $x_B = 150$ and $x_C = 350$. Alternatively, the bonus could have applied to process C alone in which case a minimum would be sought for the quantity $x_C = 1000 - x_A - x_B$. Then it would be required to find the maximum value of the sum $(x_A + x_B)$ which will occur on the contour which touches the region and is furthest in the direction up and to the right. Any point along the edge *ab* would satisfy this condition and hence provide an optimal solution, i.e. any point which satisfies

$$300 \leqslant x_A \leqslant 500$$
$$x_B = 1000 - x_A$$

and

$$x_C = 0$$

Although the example is very simple it does illustrate some useful points which generally apply to most problems of production planning considered in this book. They will help substantiate a method for finding a numerical solution in cases where it is not possible to draw out the feasible region in diagram form.

(i) *The problem is linear*, specified in terms of variables whose values satisfy a set of linear constraints and stated as a process of optimization of a linear objective function. Usually, the variables will be chosen to represent the levels of operation of processes and activities in a firm, and negative values would not be meaningful. Neither would values that reach outside the technology of the firm's production and it is necessary for a statement to be made of all equality and inequality constraints imposed. This allows the workings of the 'black box' aspect of the firm to play a large part in the model and involves the technological problems of the engineer to a much greater extent than conventional economics.

There is, though, an assumption of linearity to be imposed which implies that the quantities input to and output from the activities appear in strict proportion to the levels of the activities. In fact, part of the skill in defining the problem lies in choosing the variables so that this can be done realistically. This is not always possible, as will be seen later, and often, when quantity in itself allows cost savings to be made (*economies of scale* rather than *constant returns to scale*), it is necessary to resort to the sort of non-linear programming problem already discussed for consumer behaviour. These are much more difficult to solve numerically.

In a similar way, it is useful to express the objective function as a linear combination of variable values. This is usually quite easy, for the 'best' solution will invariably be judged from an economic point of view and will involve the minimization of cost, the sum of products of buying price and quantity of goods input, or, as in the following chapter, maximization of revenue, the sum of products of selling price and quantity of goods produced. In either case, because of the proportionality mentioned above, the linearity of the objective function will follow.

(ii) *The feasible region is convex* (A8). A production plan involves the choice of a particular combination of levels of activities. In the ex-

Production Planning

ample there were two quantities to define the eventual plan, and the feasible region describing the range of decisions could be represented on a two-dimensional diagram. Usually there will be more variables and hence the picture will contain more dimensions. The linearity of the constraints, though, will still cause the feasible region to retain its property of convexity. This will prove an important property from the point of view of systematic searches for optimal points because it means that it is possible to move along straight lines from one point to another without violating any production constraints. In other terms this implies that, once a boundary has been hit in a particular direction, there is no reason to search any further along that line.

(iii) *The optimal point lies on the boundary of the feasible region.* If the selection of an optimal point is made on the basis of the flat plane contours (A10) of the objective function, then that point will be found at the edge of the region. This would be expected, for optimality means following a direction to the extremity of the region and any point that lies completely inside the constraints could be superseded by another point lying further in that direction. This is a significant property, for any search need only be confined to the boundary. In fact, because the objective function is linear and therefore as 'flat' as the edges of the region, it is only necessary to examine the vertices. If a point in the middle of an edge is optimal, then so will be the vertices at the ends of that edge.

(iv) *At a vertex there are at least as many constraints exactly met as there are variables in the problem.* In the example there were three variables x_A, x_B and x_C whose values had to be determined. The introduction of the production target placed an equality constraint on the freedom of choice of the values, and only two variables were necessary in the search for an optimum. The problem had two *degrees of freedom* in its solution. If, instead, two constraints had been equalities, a further degree of freedom would have been lost and the search made in terms of whichever final variable was selected. The introduction of a third equality would remove all freedom and the production possibilities would be reduced to a single point.

In tackling the problem the freedom could have been expressed by any selection of two variables. If x_A and x_C had been chosen, say, then the inequality constraints would have looked different and been equivalent to a complete transformation of Fig. 3.1 into another pair of dimensions. The final answers, though, would have been the same. Usually, the variables selected at any time to describe the problem are referred to as *independent variables*. It is often convenient, because of the change in geometrical interpretation, to change the composition of the set of these variables during computation. This will involve using the equality constraints to substitute combinations of the new variables and those remaining, for the retiring variables. Thus, to change independent variables from (x_A, x_B) to (x_A, x_C) it would have been necessary to use the formula

$$x_B = 1000 - x_A - x_C$$

in all the inequality constraints.

At a vertex the remaining freedom of decision is reduced to a point. Each inequality constraint in the geometrical representation describes either part of the boundary of the feasible region or otherwise is superseded by another constraint, and hence is *redundant*. (An example is the line $1000 - x_A - x_B = 900$ in Fig. 3.1 which does not play a part in defining the region *abcd*.) Of these two types of constraint there will be at least as many exactly met at each vertex as there are degrees of freedom, and the co-ordinates of the point fully specified. For example, in the two-dimensional diagram in Fig. 3.1 there were two edges intersecting at a vertex and each represented one constraint that was exactly met. The specific combination of quantities associated with the point was obtained by solving the equations. This gave, in general, a *basic solution*. (Mathematically, such a solution need not exist for, say, the edges might be parallel. There will usually, though, be a practical interpretation, such as the larger the quantities the 'better' the combination.)

A final remark is that not all vertices need lie in the feasible region. For one that does, the binding constraints will provide a solution that also satisfies the remaining inequalities. Such a set of variable values forms a *basic feasible solution* and the search for an optimum could be greatly simplified by a systematic examination of such points as these. This in essence is what the Simplex method, described in the next chapter, does.

3.2 Activity Analysis

In practice it is not always possible for a firm to reorganize itself to such an extent that it can move in one step to an optimal solution. It is more likely that it would want to shift from a sub-optimal position in the direction of an 'improvement' by small degrees. In a world where prices and technology remained static this would eventually lead to the 'best' production plan. Whereas the entrepreneur might otherwise use a life's experience of the results of trial and error adjustments, it is intended here to use the mathematical properties of the interdependence of the firm's activities to recommend short-cuts. The framework adopted for the exercise is known as *activity analysis* which can be introduced here also for later use in the more general description of production.

Production Planning

In the last section the description of the technology of production was reduced to a set of constraints on the levels of a number of processes. In a more generalized framework the whole range of production possibilities could be represented by a set of activities $A_j, j = 1 \ldots n$, operated at non-negative levels x_j. The constraints could be formed by interpreting different aspects, e.g. floorspace, manpower or even wear and tear on capital equipment, as a series of goods $Y_i, i = 1 \ldots m$, which are either inputs or outputs to the activities. The term 'goods' is used to represent anything that can be quantified and exhibits a proportional relationship with the level of activity. The quantity of goods involved can therefore be denoted by the product $a_{ij}x_j$ where the sign of the coefficient indicates whether good Y_i is produced or consumed in activity A_j. By convention, a positive sign indicates a net output, and a negative sign a net input.

The problem can be described by an *activity table* drawn on the lines of Table 3.1. There, the array of production coefficients a_{ij} is

TABLE 3.1
The layout of an activity table specifying the technology of production

Names of goods	Units	Market prices	Activities				Sign $\geqslant, =, \leqslant$ or blank	Stipulations
			A_1	A_2	.....	A_n		
Y_1	...	p_1	a_{11}	a_{12}	.....	a_{1n}	$\geqslant$	b_1
Y_2	...	p_2	a_{21}	a_{22}	.....	a_{2n}	$\geqslant$	b_2
.		.	.	.		.		.
.		.	.	.		.		.
.		.	.	.		.		.
.		.	.	.		.		.
.		.	.	.		.		.
Y_m	...	p_m	a_{m1}	a_{m2}	.....	a_{mn}		b_m
		Levels:	x_1	x_2	.....	x_n		

$$\text{Maximize} \sum_{i=1}^{m} \sum_{j=1}^{n} p_i a_{ij} x_j, \quad x_j \geqslant 0$$

bordered by the market prices p_i of the goods, the levels of activity x_j, and stipulations b_i for the quantities of goods produced or consumed. The rows describe how a good fits into the production activities, and contain entries in the market prices column according to the cost of buying or selling that good. They also contain values for the coefficients to indicate how it is used or produced in the production activities, and entries in the stipulation column according to the constraints imposed on the quantities produced. A good Y_i that is produced at a fixed target level will have an equality and a positive stipulation in the last column, while one that is consumed up to a fixed quantity has an inequality and that quantity placed there with a minus sign. If there is a ceiling on production, then an inequality and the limit are entered, and, if there is no constraint on the good, the stipulation column is left empty. Finally, the objective function is calculated from the total revenue obtained and will therefore be

$$\sum_{j=1}^{n}\left(\sum_{i=1}^{m} p_i a_{ij}\right) x_j = \sum_{i=1}^{m}\sum_{j=1}^{n} p_i a_{ij} x_j$$

For illustration, one of the bonus problems of the last section is written out in Table 3.2 where non-entries indicate zero values in all

TABLE 3.2

An activity table used to describe the problem of minimizing bonus payments in casing production

Goods	Units	Market prices	Activities				Stipulations
			A	B	C		
Casings	casings		1	1	1	$=$	1000
Capacity A	casings/week		-1			$\geqslant$	-500
Capacity B	casings/week			-1		$\geqslant$	-700
Capacity C	casings/week				-1	$\geqslant$	-900
Floor area	sq ft		-5	-10	-16	$\geqslant$	-9600
Man-weeks	bonuses	1			-1		
			x_A	x_B	x_C		

Maximize $-x_C$, $x_A, x_B, x_C, \geqslant 0$

Production Planning

but the last column. Four of the constraints were originally 'less than or equal to' but, because the production coefficients for the capacity of plant and for floor area are negative, the signs are reversed to read 'greater than or equal to'.

3.3 Searching for Improvement

The information contained in the activity table can be used to indicate how a firm might 'best' make small changes in the organization of production. Once the current production figures are known, they can be viewed within the framework of constraints and a suggestion made as to the largest immediate improvement. This can be obtained by altering the activity levels x_j and making a judgement on the basis of the effect on the value of the objective function. The detailed advice will depend on how the current position $(x_1^1, x_2^1, \ldots x_n^1)$ fits into the constraints and, to help the discussion, it will be useful to reorganize the table.

There are four changes to make. Firstly, the equality constraints can be used to eliminate as many variables as possible. Although this will reduce the number of columns in the table, it will not affect the number of constraint lines for the previous equality constraint will be replaced by an inequality expressing the requirement that the eliminated variable cannot be negative. The exercise has effectively been carried out already in the example of casing production when the problem was rephrased in terms of the two variables x_A and x_B. Secondly, to simplify the table, the non-constraint lines are replaced by one line describing the objective function and, thirdly, any goods associated with the lines in which there are 'less than or equal to' constraints are redefined so that the constraints read 'greater than or equal to'. Finally, constants in the right-hand stipulation column are reversed in sign.

As a result of the changes, the elements of the new table can be totalled across the rows to give the sum of products of production coefficients and activity levels together with the right-hand constant which, in all, is equal to the slack associated with the constraint. This can be emphasized by defining another set of variables which will be referred to as *slack variables*. Where a_{ij} is the production coefficient of the independent variable in the ith constraint of the new table, these new variables can be denoted by $x_j, j = n, n+1, \ldots n+m$ and defined by

$$x_{n+i} \equiv \sum_{j=1}^{n} a_{ij} x_j + b_i, i = 1, \ldots m$$

where b_i are the new constant values. The objective function can be denoted by

$$\sum_{j=1}^{n} c_j x_j + c$$

where the constants c_j and c are, by definition, the result of substitutions made in the original objective function. For the example, the new table is shown in Table 3.3. It can be seen that the slack variables have

TABLE 3.3
The condensed activity table showing the values of the slack variables for two points in the feasible region

	Slack variable		Independent variables $x_A \geqslant 0 \mid x_B \geqslant 0$		Constant		Col. X	Col. Y
Process C	x_C	=	−1	−1	+1000	⩾0	100	50
Excess capacity A	x_D	=	−1		+500	⩾0	275	250
Excess capacity B	x_E	=		−1	+700	⩾0	25	0
Excess capacity C	x_F	=	+1	+1	−100	⩾0	800	850
Spare floor area	x_G	=	+11	+6	−6400	⩾0	125	550
	Maximize		+1	+1	−1000		−100	−50

different meanings in the problem. For the first row the variable is the level of process C, for the next three rows they are the excess production capacity on each of the processes, and for the last row the spare floor area. They can all be evaluated from the two independent variables x_A and x_B which together take up fully the degrees of freedom in the production plan.

From the point of view of computation, the simplest advice can be given to a firm which is operating at an interior point in the feasible region. Then, none of the inequalities are met and all variables are strictly positive. An example is production of casings in the mix $(x_A, x_B) = (225, 675)$ for which the slack variables adopt the values in column X in Table 3.3. From the discussions of the last section it will

Production Planning

be clear that the firm will not be at an optimum and it would be useful to know what direction would provide the greatest immediate improvement in terms of the objective function.

Denote a small move by increments dx_j in the independent variables x_j and suppose that the new position is never more than a distance d away from the original position. The 'best' immediate improvement can then be found by minimizing the function $\sum_{j=1}^{n} c_j dx_j + c$ subject to the constraint

$$d^2 = \sum_{j=1}^{n} dx_j^2$$

(This equation is derived by applying Pythagoras' Theorem.) For the example of casing production, Fig. 3.3 shows the new position re-

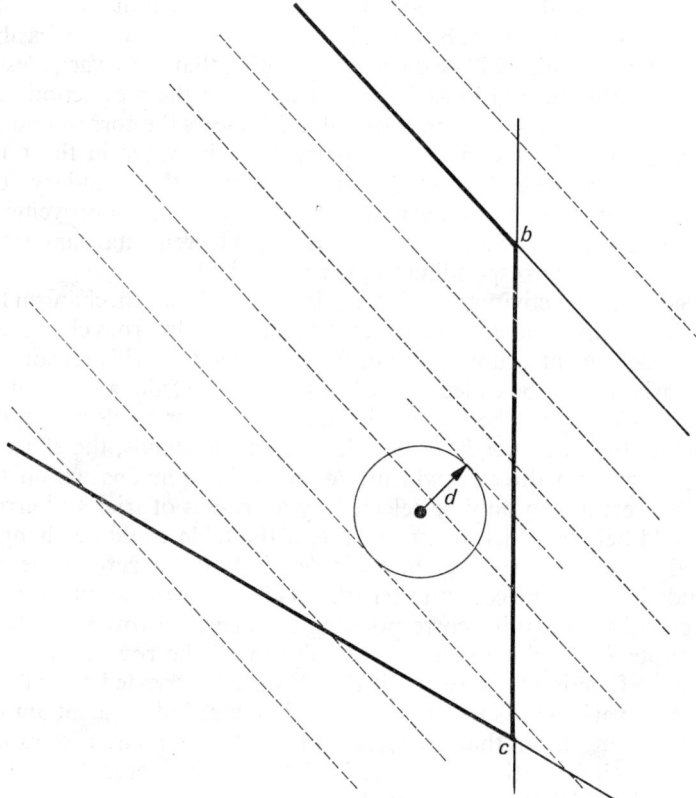

Fig. 3.3 Scope for a move of distance d from a point inside the feasible region.

stricted to a circle round the old position, and the 'best' direction lies at right angles to the broken contour lines. In the general case, this direction can be described, using the method of Lagrange multipliers (A13), by the equations

$$c_j - 2\lambda\, dx_j = 0, j = 1 \ldots n$$

for some single value λ. In other words, the advice for an immediate 'improvement' is to choose the increments in the independent variables in proportion to the coefficients of the new objective function. Therefore, working from the split $(x_A, x_B) = (225, 675)$ the firm would increase production through processes A and B in the ratio 1 : 1 at the expense of process C. Of course, such a direction can only be exploited up to a boundary, until one of the original inequality constraints is met, and the corresponding slack variable becomes zero. In this case it will be at a point $(x_A, x_B, x_C) = (250, 700, 50)$.

Suppose now that the firm is at a position where a number of the inequality constraints are binding, i.e. on the boundary of the feasible region. Such a point will be detected by noting that some variables of the new table are zero in value. For example, in the production mix $(x_A, x_B) = (250, 700)$ column Y of Table 3.3 shows the corresponding values for the slack variables. In particular, the value in the third row is zero, $x_E = 0$. Clearly, for such a point on the boundary, it is not always possible to follow a direction of maximum improvement. The question arises of the effect on subsequent incremental changes of the constraints corresponding to the zero variables.

A condensed activity table like Table 3.3 provides a mechanism for deriving the incremental changes in the row variables from changes in their independent counterparts in the columns. (For this reason the row variables can be called *dependent*.) Any move from a position on the boundary must be made with care so as not to decrease any variables that are already zero and, as the table stands, the effect of changes are not directly evident. A move that remains within the feasible region can only be selected by a process of trial and error. It would help considerably, therefore, if the table could be changed round temporarily so that the variables that take a zero value are included among the column variables. This can be achieved by using the equality constraint corresponding to each zero row variable to substitute for positive column variables in all the rows and in the objective function. The result, if the process is repeated for all the zero row variables, is to mix variables that were independent among the rows, and those that are slack among the columns. It does not change the information contained in the table, but merely rearranges the way in which it is represented.

Carrying out the transformation in the example of the production

Production Planning

mix $(x_A, x_B) = (250, 700)$, the positive column variable x_B can be replaced by the zero variable x_E. For the third row these two variables exchange places over the equals sign and, as the coefficient of x_B is then unity, the row coefficients and constant remains the same. As far as other rows and the objective function are concerned, the substitution

$$x_B = -x_E + 700$$

transforms the table values to those in Table 3.4. On the right-hand

TABLE 3.4
The condensed activity table after substitution for the independent variable x_B from the slack variable x_E

Row variables		Column variables		Constant		Col. Y
		$x_A \geqslant 0$	$x_E \geqslant 0$			
x_C	=	-1	$+1$	$+300$	$\geqslant 0$	50
x_D	=	-1		$+500$	$\geqslant 0$	250
x_B	=		-1	$+700$	$\geqslant 0$	700
x_F	=	$+1$	-1	$+600$	$\geqslant 0$	850
x_G	=	$+11$	-6	-2200	$\geqslant 0$	550
Maximize		$+1$	-1	-300		-50

side an extra column, column Y, has been added as a check that when the position $(x_A, x_E) = (250, 0)$ is substituted into the equations, the remaining variables still take the same values.

Although the example is an easy enough problem to manipulate, it may not always be possible to confine zero variables to the columns. This will happen when the point lies on more constraints than there are degrees of freedom to the problem, i.e. more than n variables equal to zero at the same time. There are generally two ways out. Firstly, it is possible to derive the 'best' direction for improvement without consideration of the rows that are left with zero variables, and then check for a violation of the requirement that those variables remain non-negative. If they do, then the direction will still be the best possible when the constraints are reintroduced. Otherwise, the zero variable rows and columns can be interchanged, the test repeated and eventually by trial and error the possibility of a change in the firm's position established. Secondly, it is possible to perturb slightly the set of original constraints by adding a series of powers of a very small value to the right-hand constants. The value must be small relative to values in the activity table. The effect will be to break the coincidence of the equations and hence take away the possibility of so many zero variables. In this particular situation, though, much care would be required in the interpretation of the result, for, in slightly distorting the problem, a direction could be opened up in which it might only be possible to move a very small distance. Another table would then have to be constructed and the direction reviewed.

The advantage of the reorganization is that the choice of direction is made by consideration of only the column variables. Whatever changes are contemplated, the positive row variables will not immediately become negative. It is only the zero-valued column variables that must not be decreased. For such variables it will only be possible to follow the preferred direction if the incremental change is non-negative, i.e. the coefficient in the objective function is non-negative. The rule becomes that the best direction is denoted by increments that are proportional to the coefficients of the objective function unless a particular coefficient is negative and the corresponding column variable has zero value. If the objective function in the rearranged table is denoted by $\sum_j c_j' x_j$ with coefficients c_j', then the incremental change dx_j for column variable x_j is given in terms of a positive value d by

$$dx_j = \begin{cases} c_j'd \text{ if } x_j > 0 \\ \max(c_j'd, 0) \text{ if } x_j = 0 \end{cases}$$

and for row variable x_i by

$$dx_i = \sum_j a_{ij}' dx_j$$

where a_{ij}' is the array of coefficients for the rearranged table.

3.4 The Optimal Position

There is, of course, the possibility that the firm is already at the 'best' production position. This would be indicated by all the increments derived above being equal to zero and can occur if either the value of the coefficient c_j' is zero or negative. In the first case, although the original constraint associated with the variable is not necessarily binding, no change that might be made will affect the value of the objective function. Such a point could be one of a series of multiple solutions all of which provide a 'best' combination. On the other hand, in the second case, the zero increment will result from the

Production Planning

column variable x_j being zero and hence one of the original constraints exactly met.

In the example, where the firm is at a point $(x_A, x_E) = (250, 0)$ the preferred direction would be such that $dx_A = d$ and $dx_E = -d$ for some positive value d. As the value of variable x_E is zero, however, the best that can be achieved will be $dx_A = d$ and $dx_E = 0$. This is a move along the constraint associated with the slack variable x_E, i.e. the line bc in Fig. 3.1. The direction can be pursued up to the point b where $x_A = 300$ and $x_E = 0$ which is an optimal position. The optimality can be checked by noting that the two variables x_C and x_E will then be zero and, when the column variable x_A is replaced by the row variable x_C, the objective function becomes simply $-x_C$ with coefficients -1 and 0. The increments equal zero, $dx_C = dx_E = 0$, and the combination $(x_A, x_B, x_C) = (300, 700, 0)$ is an optimum.

4 Computation and Valuation

In the last chapter a framework was developed for the analysis of production problems, and some indications obtained about where the optimal solutions lie and how they might be identified. The example took a simple short-term approach of minimizing cost with fixed outputs. It is possible now to take a broader standpoint and look at methods for actually evaluating the optimal solution in a more comprehensive, but still short-term, problem of maximizing net revenue. The discussion will start with *the Simplex method*, due to G. B. Dantzig. This is probably the most widely known algorithm in linear programming and will not only cope with the short term but will also help establish principles for making economic valuations that are suitable for longer term management decisions.

4.1 The Simplex Method

Consider a firm producing three chemicals, C_1, C_2, and C_3 from input combinations of two of them, C_2 and C_3 by the operation of plants P_1, P_2 and P_3. Suppose that the management objective is to maximize net revenue, the balance of sales revenue and production cost, with the stipulation that the firm is already committed to its supplies of chemicals C_2 and C_3. This, together with the virtual lack of flexibility in the use of plant, characterizes the problem as a short-term one. The production itself involves a combination of the following four activities:

A_1, production of C_1 in plant P_1 using the workforce on regular time. The unit plant operation cost of £1.00 and capacity 4000 units per week. Chemicals C_2 and C_3 are required for input.

A_2, production of C_1 in stand-by plant P_2 using the workforce on regular time. The unit plant operation cost is £0.25 and capacity 1000 units per week. Input C_2 and C_3.

A_3, production of C_1 in plant P_1 using the workforce on overtime. The unit plant operation cost is £3.00 and capacity 1000 per week. Input C_2 and C_3.

A_4, joint production of C_2 and C_3 in plant P_3 at a plant operation cost of £3.00 with a capacity 5000 units per week. Input C_2.

Computation and Valuation

The actual production coefficients are described in the activity table, Table 4.1, where two activities, A_5 and A_6, are added to distri-

TABLE 4.1
Activity table for chemical firm

Goods	Market price	Activities						Stipulation	
		A_1	A_2	A_3	A_4	A_5	A_6		
Sales C_1	4	+3	+2	+3				$\geq$	0
Stock C_2		−2	−2	−2	−1	+1			0
Bought C_2	4					−1		=	−15000
Stock C_3		−1	−2	−1	+2		+1	$\geq$	0
Bought C_3	2						−1	=	−6000
Capacity P_1 regular		−1						$\geq$	−4000
Capacity P_1 overtime				−1				$\geq$	−1000
Capacity P_2			−1					$\geq$	−1000
Capacity P_3					−1			$\geq$	−5000
Direct costs	1	−1	−0·25	−3	−3				
Maximize		+11	+7·75	+9	−3	−4	−2		

bute the fixed supplies of chemicals C_2 and C_3 between their various uses. They make it possible for some of the chemicals to be left over in spite of the fact that cost is worked out from total supply. Chemical C_1, on the other hand, can always be sold at £4.00 per unit and the buying prices of chemicals C_2 and C_3 are £4.00 and £2.00 per unit respectively. These prices are multiplied by the production coefficients in each column to give the objective function coefficients which will then be sufficient to indicate the direct influence of the activity levels on net revenue. The computation procedure has to find a set of zero or positive activity levels that provide the largest value of this function and at the same time satisfy the eight constraints in the table.

The Simplex method searches for an optimum by examining only the basic feasible solutions. As mentioned in the last chapter, at least one of these will be an optimal point. The algorithm starts by finding a vertex inside the feasible region and then makes moves along the edges to more favourable vertices until a 'best' point has been reached. Because the feasible region is bounded by a finite number of flat planes, each corresponding to a constraint, there is at most a fixed number of vertices to examine. The algorithm ensures that the optimum will be reached after a finite number of steps.

It will be important therefore to find the first basic feasible solution and establish a method of moving to the next and so on. Each time there has to be as many binding constraints as there are degrees of freedom, and subsequent changes require replacement of one or more of them by others. This type of manipulation was carried out in the last chapter and it will be convenient to begin from the same condensed tableau. By removing the equality constraints in Table 4.1 by substitution, retaining only the 'greater than or equal to' inequality constraint rows, negating the right-hand stipulation column and, finally, introducing new variables to take up the slack in the row constraints, Table 4.2 can be obtained. This divides the variables into two groups, row variables and column variables, the last of which are as numerous as the degrees of freedom. If, therefore, those variables are set to zero, there will be as many constraints binding, either as row constraints or simply as requirements for non-negative values, as there are degrees of freedom, and hence the corresponding point will be a vertex. Any subsequent change to another vertex would require the replacement of one or more column variables by row variables which are themselves set to zero. This is a procedure that is already familiar from the last chapter.

In the example the initial question will be whether the simplified tableau of Table 4.2 with column variables set to zero provides a basic feasible solution and is thus a suitable starting point for the Simplex algorithm. In fact, if the variables x_1, x_2, x_3 and x_4 are set to zero, all the other variables, x_5, x_6, . . . x_{12}, are strictly positive, and hence $(x_1, x_2, x_3, x_4) = (0, 0, 0, 0)$ represents a vertex that lies in the feasible region. By way of terminology, because they are zero, the four column variables are, at this stage, called *non-basic* and the eight row variables which depend on them *basic*. (The convention used for the signs of the production coefficients in Table 4.2 turns out to be different to that usually found in the Simplex tableau. This has arisen because of the convention of 'positive coefficients for outputs and negative for inputs' and the layout inherited from the last chapter where the dependant variable is put equal to the sum, along each row, of the products of production coefficients and activity levels added to the stipulation constant. For the sake of consistency throughout the book, the convention of Table 4.2 will be retained).

It may not always be possible to reach a situation where putting all the column variables to zero causes all the row variables to be strictly positive. Some of the row variables might be negative, or zero. If they are negative, the basic solution is not feasible. To rectify the situation

TABLE 4.2
Condensed activity table for the chemical firm

Goods		Activities A_1 $x_1 \geqslant 0$	A_2 $x_2 \geqslant 0$	A_3 $x_3 \geqslant 0$	A_4 $x_4 \geqslant 0$	Constant
A_5	$x_5 =$					$+15000 \geqslant 0$
A_6	$x_6 =$					$+6000 \geqslant 0$
Spare C_2	$x_7 =$	-2	-2	-2	-1	$+15000 \geqslant 0$
Spare C_3	$x_8 =$	-1	-2	-1	$+2$	$+6000 \geqslant 0$
Spare capacity P_1 regular	$x_9 =$	-1				$+4000 \geqslant 0$
Spare capacity P_1 overtime	$x_{10} =$			-1		$+1000 \geqslant 0$
Spare capacity P_2	$x_{11} =$		-1			$+1000 \geqslant 0$
Spare capacity P_3	$x_{12} =$				-1	$+5000 \geqslant 0$
Maximize		$+11$	$+7\cdot75$	$+9$	-3	-72000

an extra activity can be introduced with production coefficients set to -1 on every row that has a negative value, and with a very large negative coefficient $-M$ in the objective function. By choosing the level of this activity equal in size to the largest negative constant in the right-hand column, the corresponding row variable will be brought to a zero value. If a substitution is now made so that this row replaces the extra activity column, a solution will be reached where at least there will be no negative row variables. So the immediate problem of the non-feasible vertex is avoided, and as long as the value M is large enough, the extra activity would be expected to be too costly to enter the final solution at anything but a zero level. Hence the result of the optimization would not be affected. If the extra activity did not disappear, however, then no feasible solution exists at all.

Alternatively, if some of the row variables are zero while the rest are positive, the basic solution is feasible but over-identified in terms of constraint equations. This situation has been met in the last chapter and there are again two possible way of coping with it. Firstly, every combination of zero variables could be tried in the columns in the hope that either a feasible improvement is found, or otherwise an optimum acknowledged. Secondly, a perturbation could be made to all the constraints to destroy the coincidence of the constraint planes. Either way, the aim is to make a positive move away from the troublesome vertex. Once this has been achieved there is no need to return.

Having established an initial start, the computation attempts to move amongst the vertices each time improving the value of the objective function. The rules for this are simple and can be deduced directly from the previous chapter. If coefficients of the objective function in the current stage are all negative or zero, then a maximum has been reached. Otherwise, if some coefficients are positive, then an increase in the corresponding column variable would lead to an increase in the value of the objective function whilst, initially at least, no variable, row or column, would have to become negative. By convention, the column variable with the largest positive coefficient is chosen and increased until one of the row variables becomes zero. When this occurs the row variable is accepted into the non-basic set and the column variable displaced to the basic set. A new feasible vertex will have been found, and the table prepared for the examination of the new objective function coefficients. (If all the production coefficients in the column had been non-negative, the variable can be increased indefinitely without any row variables becoming negative. This indicates that the objective function can be increased without limit by the expansion of certain activities.)

In the example, Table 4.2 has a coefficient $+11$ in the objective function. If the corresponding variable x_1 is increased, the variable x_9, which originally had value $+4000$, is reduced to zero before the other row variables. It will therefore be chosen to join the non-basic variables while the variable x_1 is made basic. The table can be rearranged by substituting

$$x_1 = -x_9 + 4000$$

throughout.

A standard procedure for exchanging the variables is known as the *pivotal method*. If, say, the column variable x_j is to be replaced by the row variable x_i, then the (i,j)th element is denoted as the *pivot*, the jth column (including the objective function coefficient) as the *pivot column*, and the ith row (including the right-hand constant) as the *pivot row*. For the substitution,

(i) replace the pivot by its reciprocal,
(ii) divide other elements in the pivot column by the old pivot,
(iii) negate other elements in the pivot row and divide by the old pivot, and
(iv) subtract from the remaining elements (s,t) the cross-product of old elements (s,j) and (i,t) divided by the old pivot.

(The pivotal method usually appears different because of an alternative choice of table layout. The pivot column elements and not the row elements are then negated before manipulation.) The first tableau in Table 4.3 has the pivot, valued -1, ringed and, when inverted, this again gives -1. The other elements in the first column are divided by -1 and in the fifth row by $+1$. From all other elements, e.g. $+15\,000$ which is the entry in the right-hand column opposite variable x_7, the appropriate cross-product is subtracted to give

$$15\,000 - \frac{(-2)(4000)}{-1} = 7000$$

As a general rule for deciding on the pivot, the column with the largest positive coefficient in the current objective function can be used for the pivotal column. Then, the production coefficient is chosen in this column which gives the smallest value when it is divided by the stipulation constant currently in the same row. (If the constant is zero, then it is supposedly replaced by a very small positive value.) The coefficient would be expected to be negative. It then becomes the pivot and the row in which it lies the pivotal row. If, otherwise, the coefficient were non-negative, the variable associated with the potential pivotal column could be increased indefinitely and no actual maximum value would exist.

The moves are repeated until a final optimal solution is reached. For the example, the steps are described in Table 4.3 where the pivot elements are ringed. There, the changes are not all that surprising. They gradually open up the production processes until the three most profitable processes, P_1, P_2 and P_3, are expanded up to capacity. The process P_4 is used only as much as is necessary to provide a sufficient quantity of the chemical C_2 for the other processes.

4.2 Derivation of the Supply Curve

If the chemical firm is to sell to consumers, it will be interesting to look at the optimization of net revenue for different prices of chemical C_1. Suppose the price is £p per unit, then the final solution found in Table 4.3 will not necessarily be optimal. In fact, according to the value of p, there will be different final tableaux. The objective function coefficients for them are given in Table 4.4 where each line corresponds to a range of values of the price p. Noticeably, they will all be negative or zero for the range specified, and, as would be expected, for the higher selling prices the solution calls more on the less profitable production processes.

TABLE 4.3
The succession of tableaux leading to an optimum for the chemical firm

1st tableau	x_1	x_2	x_3	x_4	
x_5					+15000
x_6					+6000
x_7	-2	-2	-2	-1	+15000
x_8	-1	-2	-1	$+2$	+6000
x_9	$\boxed{-1}$				+4000
x_{10}			-1		+1000
x_{11}		-1			+1000
x_{12}				-1	+5000
Maximize	$+11$	$+7{\cdot}75$	$+9$	-3	-72000

2nd tableau	x_9	x_2	x_3	x_4	
x_5					+15000
x_6					+6000
x_7	$+2$	-2	-2	-1	+7000
x_8	$+1$	-2	-1	$+2$	+2000
x_1	-1				+4000
x_{10}			$\boxed{-1}$		+1000
x_{11}		-1			+1000
x_{12}				-1	+5000
Maximize	-11	$+7{\cdot}75$	$+9$	-3	-28000

TABLE 4.3 (*continued*)

3rd tableau

	x_9	x_2	x_{10}	x_4	
x_5					$+15000$
x_6					$+6000$
x_7	$+2$	-2	$+2$	-1	$+5000$
x_8	$+1$	$\boxed{-2}$	$+1$	$+2$	$+1000$
x_1	-1				$+4000$
x_3			-1		$+1000$
x_{11}		-1			$+1000$
x_{12}				-1	$+5000$
Maximize	-11	$+7\cdot75$	-9	-3	-19000

4th tableau

	x_9	x_8	x_{10}	x_4	
x_5					$+15000$
x_6					$+6000$
x_7	$+1$	$+1$	$+1$	-3	$+4000$
x_2	$+0\cdot5$	$-0\cdot5$	$+0\cdot5$	$+1$	$+500$
x_1	-1				$+4000$
x_3			-1		$+1000$
x_{11}	$-0\cdot5$	$+0\cdot5$	$-0\cdot5$	$\boxed{-1}$	$+500$
x_{12}				-1	$+5000$
Maximize	$-7\cdot125$	$-3\cdot875$	$-5\cdot125$	$+4\cdot75$	-15125

5th tableau

	x_9	x_8	x_{10}	x_{11}	
x_5					$+15000$
x_6					$+6000$
x_7	$+2\cdot5$	$-0\cdot5$	$+2\cdot5$	$+3$	$+2500$
x_2				-1	$+1000$
x_1	-1				$+4000$
x_3			-1		$+1000$
x_4	$-0\cdot5$	$+0\cdot5$	$-0\cdot5$	-1	$+500$
x_{12}	$+0\cdot5$	$-0\cdot5$	$+0\cdot5$	$+1$	$+4500$
Maximize	$-9\cdot5$	$-1\cdot5$	$-7\cdot5$	$-4\cdot75$	-12750

TABLE 4.4
Objective function coefficients for the optimal position in the chemical firm example with different ranges of price, p for chemical C_1

Price range	Non-basic variables in the optimal solution and their coefficients				Maximum revenue
$0 \leqslant p \leqslant 0.125$	x_1	x_2	x_3	x_4	-72000
	$-1 + 3p$	$-0.25 + 2p$	$-3 + 3p$	-3	
$0.125 \leqslant p \leqslant 0.333$	x_1	x_{11}	x_3	x_4	-72250
	$-1 + 3p$	$0.25 - 2p$	$-3 + 3p$	-3	$+2000p$
$0.333 \leqslant p \leqslant 1.000$	x_9	x_{11}	x_3	x_4	-76250
	$1 - 3p$	$0.25 - 2p$	$-3 + 3p$	-3	$+14000p$
$1.000 \leqslant p \leqslant 1.438$	x_9	x_{11}	x_8	x_4	-76250
	-2	$-5.75 + 4p$	$3 - 3p$	$-9 + 6p$	$+14000p$
$1.438 \leqslant p \leqslant 1.625$	x_9	x_{10}	x_8	x_4	-79125
	$0.875 - 2p$	$2.875 - 2p$	$0.125 - p$	$3.25 - 2p$	$+16000p$
$1.625 \leqslant p$	x_9	x_{10}	x_8	x_{11}	-80750
	$2.5 - 3p$	$4.5 - 3p$	-1.5	$3.25 - 2p$	$+17000p$

Computation and Valuation

Expressing the difference between the optima in terms of quantity of chemical C_1 produced against price, Fig. 4.1 traces out what is usually called the *supply curve*, the amount of a good that a firm is prepared to supply at a given price. In the case considered here, only short-term decisions are taken and the curve applies to changes that can take place over short spans of time. In practice the curve will virtually always be either level or upward-rising showing that, as

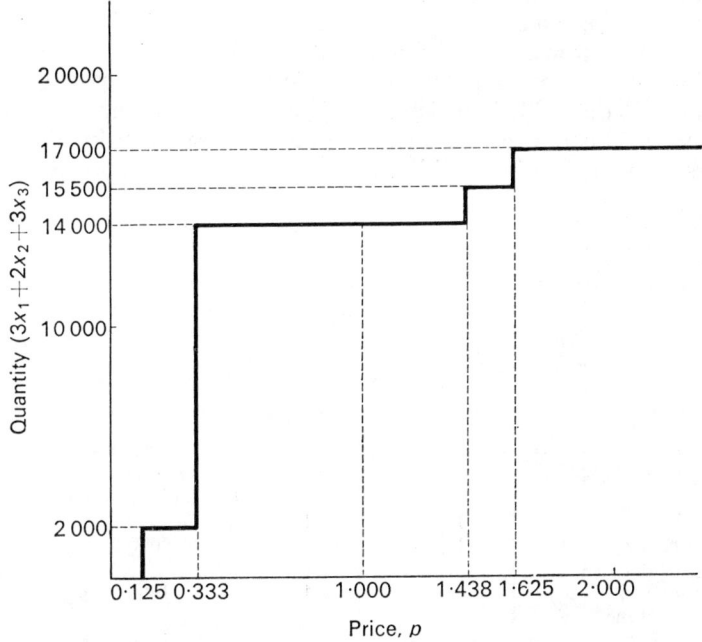

Fig. 4.1 Short-term supply curve of chemical C_1.

price increases the less profitable processes are brought into action. The existence of the curve proves to be an important parallel between traditional economics and the treatment of production planning by mathematical programming. The only difference is that where in the first case the supply curve is expected to be smooth, in the second it is described by a series of straight lines. This really is only a question of the degree of aggregation and the coarseness of the description of the technology. Once supply curves are added together in a description of the quantity sold by a collection of firms, and once the distinction between production activities is reduced, the straight lines become more numerous and the corners less severe.

4.3 Valuation at the Margin

So far the approach has placed economic objectives onto an engineering problem. A major contribution of linear programming is that this enables a value framework to be added. An account can be drawn up to break down the net revenue into a list of values that can be associated with the rows of the activity table. Therefore, in addition to the actual market prices, there will be a set of *imputed valuations* to place against the goods associated with the row constraints. These, it will be seen, can be turned into advice on the marginal profitability of action the firm could take in the future.

For the Simplex computation the basic activity table was converted to a condensed table in which the original non-constraint rows were dropped. This time a more elaborate table is constructed with these rows converted to inequalities. An example is Table 4.5 which is a

TABLE 4.5
An extended activity table for the chemical firm

Goods		Activities				Constant	Market prices
		A_1 $x_1 \geqslant 0$	A_2 $x_2 \geqslant 0$	A_3 $x_3 \geqslant 0$	A_4 $x_4 \geqslant 0$		
Bought C_2, A_5	$x_5 =$					$+15000 \geqslant 0$	-4
Bought C_3, A_6	$x_6 =$					$+6000 \geqslant 0$	-2
Spare C_2	$x_7 =$	-2	-2	-2	-1	$+15000 \geqslant 0$	
Spare C_3	$x_8 =$	-1	-2	-1	$+2$	$+6000 \geqslant 0$	
Spare capacity P_1 regular	$x_9 =$	-1				$+4000 \geqslant 0$	
Spare capacity P_1 overtime	$x_{10} =$			-1		$+1000 \geqslant 0$	
Spare capacity P_2	$x_{11} =$		-1			$+1000 \geqslant 0$	
Spare capacity P_3	$x_{12} =$				-1	$+5000 \geqslant 0$	
Sales C_1	$x_{13} =$	$+3$	$+2$	$+3$		$+0 \geqslant 0$	$+4$
Money (direct costs)	$x_{14} =$	$+1$	$+0.25$	$+3$	$+3$	$+0 \geqslant 0$	-1
Maximize		$+11$	$+7.75$	$+9$	-3	-72000	

repeat of Table 4.2 with information added from the original Table 4.1. It includes a column of market prices which are set to both positive and negative values. The reason for this is that the market prices, say for variables x_5 and x_6, have been applied to goods that are differently defined. Instead of originally referring to the quantity of goods C_2 and C_3 input, a negative value, they now indicate the level of buying activity, a positive value. Hence they will represent a drain on net revenue and deserve a negative price. The same argument applies to the variable x_{14}.

Denoting the production coefficients for rows i and columns j in the table by the array, a_{ij}, $i = 1, \ldots m, j = 1, \ldots n$, the constants by b_i and prices by p_i, the relationship between row and column variables can be written

$$x_{n+i} = \sum_{j=1}^{n} a_{ij}x_j + b_i, i = 1, \ldots m$$

and the objective function is derived from the equation

$$\sum_{i=1}^{m} p_i x_{n+i} = \sum_{i=1}^{m} \sum_{j=1}^{n} p_i a_{ij} x_j + \sum_{i=1}^{m} p_i b_i$$

The prices p_i are effectively a set of weights which, when applied to the values in each column of production coefficients, provide the coefficients of net revenue when it is expressed solely in terms of column variables. Therefore, while the prices provide the coefficients of the row variables in one of the expressions for net revenue, they also show how the coefficients should be combined for net revenue to be expressed in terms of the column variables.

The description of net revenue as a function of column variables is particularly useful in the definition of marginal changes. Suppose that the column variables are set to zero in, for example, Table 4.5. If the marginal changes were implemented through some of the basic variables, then the implications about other variables would be difficult to trace through the table, and they may even break the non-negative requirement. On the other hand, the non-basic variables are independent of each other and have a clear relationship with the basic variables. Together they contain all the freedom of movement that is available for marginal change from the vertex. So, for the situation in Table 4.5 where $(x_1, x_2, x_3, x_4) = (0, 0, 0, 0)$, it will be reasonable to examine marginal effects on revenue of increasing any of the variables x_1, x_2, x_3 or x_4. The result if one were changed while the others were held constant, would be the *marginal revenue* of that activity level. Therefore, for clarity, the marginal changes are taken to originate in the non-basic variables of the vertex concerned, i.e. in the column variables of the tableau. What is interesting is to look at other tableaux that arose in the search for the optimal solution. They will have a different set of non-basic variables and hence different ways of implementing marginal changes. The question that arises is of what is then implied about the value of the goods specified in the original activity table.

In the manipulations, the pivotal method was used to move from one vertex to the next and hence trace a path of stepping stones to the tableaux near the end of the computation. If, instead, a move was required directly from the first tableau to, say, the third or fifth, then, to build up the new objective function, it would be necessary to remove in one step all the new basic variables that were originally non-basic from the objective function. At the same time, all the original basic variables that remain basic must be kept out of the expression. Ideally, this manipulation would be carried out by straightforward substitution. As the original relationships between basic and non-basic variables, viz.

$$x_{n+i} = \sum_{j=1}^{n} a_{ij}x_j + b_i, i = 1, \ldots m$$

are stated as they are, however, it will be more convenient to add a suitably weighted combination of these equations to the objective function equation

$$\sum_{i=1}^{m} p_i x_{n+1} = \sum_{i=1}^{m} \sum_{j=1}^{n} p_i a_{ij} x_j + \sum_{i=1}^{m} p_i b_i$$

If the weights are denoted by $u_i, i = 1, \ldots m$, then the coefficients of the original basic variables x_{n+i} become, after the addition,

$$p_i + u_i$$

those of the original non-basic variables

$$\sum_{i=1}^{m} p_i a_{ij} + \sum_{i=1}^{m} u_i a_{ij} = \sum_{i=1}^{m} (p_i + u_i) a_{ij}$$

and the constant value

$$\sum_{i=1}^{m} p_i b_i + \sum_{i=1}^{m} u_i b_i = \sum_{i=1}^{m} (p_i + u_i) b_i$$

As a result, the new objective function equation can be written

$$\sum_{i=1}^{m} p_i x_{n+i} = -\sum_{i=1}^{m} u_i x_{n+i} + \sum_{i=1}^{m} \sum_{j=1}^{m} (p_i + u_i) a_{ij} x_j + \sum_{i=1}^{m} (p_i + u_i) b_i$$

Now, bearing in mind the variables that are to remain in the expression for net revenue, the weights u_i must be chosen so that

(i) $u_i = 0$ if the original basic variable x_{n+i} remains basic and

(ii) $\sum_{i=1}^{m} (p_i + u_i) a_{ij} = 0$ if the original non-basic variable x_j becomes basic. The objective function can then be expressed solely in terms of the new basic variables, viz.

$$\sum_{i=1}^{m} p_i x_{n+i} = -\sum_{i \in I} u_i x_{n+i} + \sum_{i=1}^{m} \sum_{j \in J} (p_i + u_i) a_{ij} x_j + \sum_{i=1}^{m} (p_i + u_i) b_i$$

where the set I contains indices of basic variables that become non-basic and J the indices of non-basic variables that remain non-basic.

The weights u_i are called *Simplex multipliers* and they help in the assessment of marginal revenues at the new vertex. Clearly, if one of the variables that have just become non-basic, x_{n+i}, $i \in I$, is given a unit increase while the other new non-basic variables are kept constant, the effect on net revenue will be an increase of size $-u_i$. (As with the sign of the value of prices, the sign of the effect will depend on whether the quantity x_{n+i} represents an input or output.) This will be made up of a direct contribution of p_i and an indirect one through changes in the basic variables that remain basic. As a result, in total terms, the marginal revenue of the quantity of the good associated with variable x_{n+i} is $-u_i$. In addition, the marginal revenue of a non-basic variable x_j for which $j \in J$ is $\sum_{i=1}^{m} (p_i + u_i) a_{ij}$. This amounts to the increase in revenue from the original basic variables net of the increase that could be attributed to those that have since become non-basic. Thus the negated Simplex multipliers have a two-fold significance. On the one hand, they give immediately the marginal revenues associated with goods whose quantity variables enter the non-basic set. On the other hand, when the activity levels that remain non-basic are changed, the multipliers help compensate for the way the alterations are implemented.

In their turn the marginal revenues associated with quantities of goods provide a system of valuation of those goods. Suppose the computation has reached an optimal solution. There will then be a split of basic and non-basic variables and a resulting set of Simplex multipliers u_i^0, $i = 1, \ldots m$. Now, if a particular variable x_{n+i} which was originally basic is non-basic in the optimal solution, the marginal revenue of the quantity x_{n+i} will be $-u_i^0$. Therefore, if the corresponding good is increased in quantity from zero to a small positive amount, the unit increase in net revenue will be u_i^0. Putting it another way, if the good in question is associated with a slack variable, e.g. spare capacity of plant, the value of the last unit of the actual good, e.g. capacity of plant, is equal to u_i^0. So the weights give a clue to the value of goods that are in limited supply at the optimum. In fact, because the Simplex multipliers have already been defined as zero for those variables that remain basic, the same can be said of the goods which have not met the quantity constraints. Hence the imputed value at the margin of the quantity x_{n+i} of any good is given by $-u_i{}^0$. Moreover, the 'net imputed value' of a unit of that good in the original allocation, remembering that it was purchased or disposed of at market price, will be $-(p_i + u_i{}^0)$.

Instead of increasing or decreasing the slack in a constraint, it is possible to think of relaxing the constant describing the actual limitation. In geometrical terms, this will be equivalent to moving a constraint line a small amount in a direction at right angles to itself. If the variable associated with the constraint is basic in the final tableau, then the alteration will not have any effect on the optimum. Revenue will change by only the price of the good, which will therefore be equal to its net imputed value. Otherwise, if it is non-basic, then, while the other non-basic variables remain zero, the change in revenue is exactly that achieved in the move by the vertex from its old position to its new one. For this to be done, production will have to be reorganized along the edge formed by the intersection of the other binding constraints, and the value $-(p_i + u_i{}^0)$ is the component of that move along the preferred direction. If only small changes are involved and the old vertex was an optimum, the shifted vertex will also be an optimum. Thus, it is possible to find a more meaningful explanation of the negated net imputed value $-(p_i + u_i{}^0)$. For the good whose quantity is described by the variable x_{n+i} it represents the change in the optimal value of net revenue if the associated constraint is relaxed.

The value of the multipliers $u_i{}^0$ can be found from the objective function row in the final Simplex tableau. For original row variables x_{n+i} that are now non-basic they are simply equal to the negated values in the appropriate columns, and for the remaining original row variables they are zero. The other values in the objective function row, those associated with original column variables, are left to represent the marginal revenues of changes in the corresponding activity levels. For the example in Table 4.3 the optimal tableau gives the imputed value of goods corresponding to variables x_8, x_9, x_{10} and x_{11} as £(−1.5), £(−9.5), £(−7.5) and £(−4.75) respectively. The first of these represents the quantity of spare chemical C_3 left over after the allocation to production activities. At the margin the chemical is costing, in imputed terms, £1.5 per unit and therefore, if it could be obtained more cheaply, there would be a case for using the alternative source of supply. As the situation stands, the fixed supply of 6000 units costs £2 per unit, and it would be worthwhile attempting to cut down this quota and relying on internal production using process A_4. In this way some spare chemical C_2 will be used. The second, third and fourth variables represent spare capacities of plant. Hence the imputed values of plant P_1, used on regular time, plant P_1 on overtime

Computation and Valuation

and plant P_2 are £9.5, £7.5 and £4.75 respectively. Obviously, increased use of plant P_1 for regular work is the most profitable single move, and the figures give the greatest additional cost that could be tolerated in the expansion.

In addition to suggestions for marginal changes, the imputed values give an alternative framework for a break-down of the firm's accounts. This can be derived by examining the objective function equation at the optimal solution, i.e. when the new non-basic variables are zero. The equation becomes

$$\sum_{i=1}^{m} p_i x_{n+i}{}^0 = \sum_{i=1}^{m} (p_i + u_i{}^0) b_i$$

and its terms are listed in Table 4.6 for each good or item that arises in the activity analysis at the optimal quantities derived in Table 4.3. On one side is a conventional list of optimal quantities of goods multiplied by their price while, on the other side, the initial allocations of goods are set against net value $(p_i + u_i{}^0)$. This sum can be used to pass judgement on the profitability of the present allocation of goods. A negative value would indicate an allocation that should be cut back, a positive value one that is worth expanding.

TABLE 4.6
A breakdown of the revenue of the chemical film

Item	Variable	Market price, p_i	Imputed value, $u_i{}^0$	Actual contribution to net revenue, $p_i x_{n+i}{}^0$			Imputed contribution to net revenue, $(p_i + u_i{}^0) b_i$		
Purchase C_2	x_5	−4		−4 ×	15000 =	−60000	−4 ×	15000 =	−60000
Purchase C_3	x_6	−2		−2 ×	6000 =	−12000	−2 ×	6000 =	−12000
Surplus C_2	x_7			0 ×	2500 =	0	0 ×	15000 =	0
Surplus C_3	x_8		1·5	0 ×	0 =	0	1·5 ×	6000 =	9000
Spare capacity P_1 regular	x_9		9·5	0 ×	0 =	0	9·5 ×	4000 =	38000
Spare capacity P_1 overtime	x_{10}		7·5	0 ×	0 =	0	7·5 ×	1000 =	7500
Spare capacity P_2	x_{11}		4·75	0 ×	0 =	0	4·75 ×	1000 =	4750
Spare capacity P_3	x_{12}			0 ×	4500 =	0	0 ×	4500 =	0
Sales C_1	x_{13}	4		4 ×	17000 =	68000	4 ×	0 =	0
Direct costs	x_{14}	−1		−1 ×	8750 =	−8750	−1 ×	0 =	0
				Total —12750			Total —12750		

One final point can be mentioned ready for the discussions of the next chapter. In the optimal solution, all coefficients in the objective function row are non-positive and hence the values $u_i{}^0$ are non-negative. Thus, for optimal values $x_{n+i}{}^0$ of all the original slack variables

$$x_{n+i}{}^0 > 0 \text{ implies } u_i{}^0 = 0$$

and
$$u_i^0 > 0 \text{ implies } x_{n+i}^0 = 0$$
In either case, $x_{n+i}^0, u_i^0 \geq 0$.

4.4 A Decomposition Algorithm

By way of a postscript to this chapter it is worth mentioning the use of imputed values to break down a large linear programme into a series of manageable sub-programmes each with its own constraints and objective function. This is called *decomposition* and is useful when the production process for the firm as a whole is complex. Then it may be better to handle the computation by treating the firm as a series of subsidiary companies that sell goods to each other and share some common facilities.

To illustrate the methodology, consider a simple example of a firm whose four production activities are given in Table 4.7. The

TABLE 4.7
The production activities of the firm and its subsidiary companies A and B

Facilities and goods	Price	Activities				Stipulations	
		A_1	A_2	B_1	B_2		
C_1		−1	−2	−2	−1	≥	−40
C_2		−1	−4			≥	−36
C_3		−2	−1			≥	−16
C_4				−1		≥	−10
C_5					−1	≥	−15
C_6				−1	−1	≥	−16
C_7	1	+3	+3	+3	+1		
Maximize		+3	+3	+3	+1		

coefficients have been arranged in a series of groups. One group lies across all the columns and the others form diagonal blocks which do not have any rows or columns in common. The first contains the

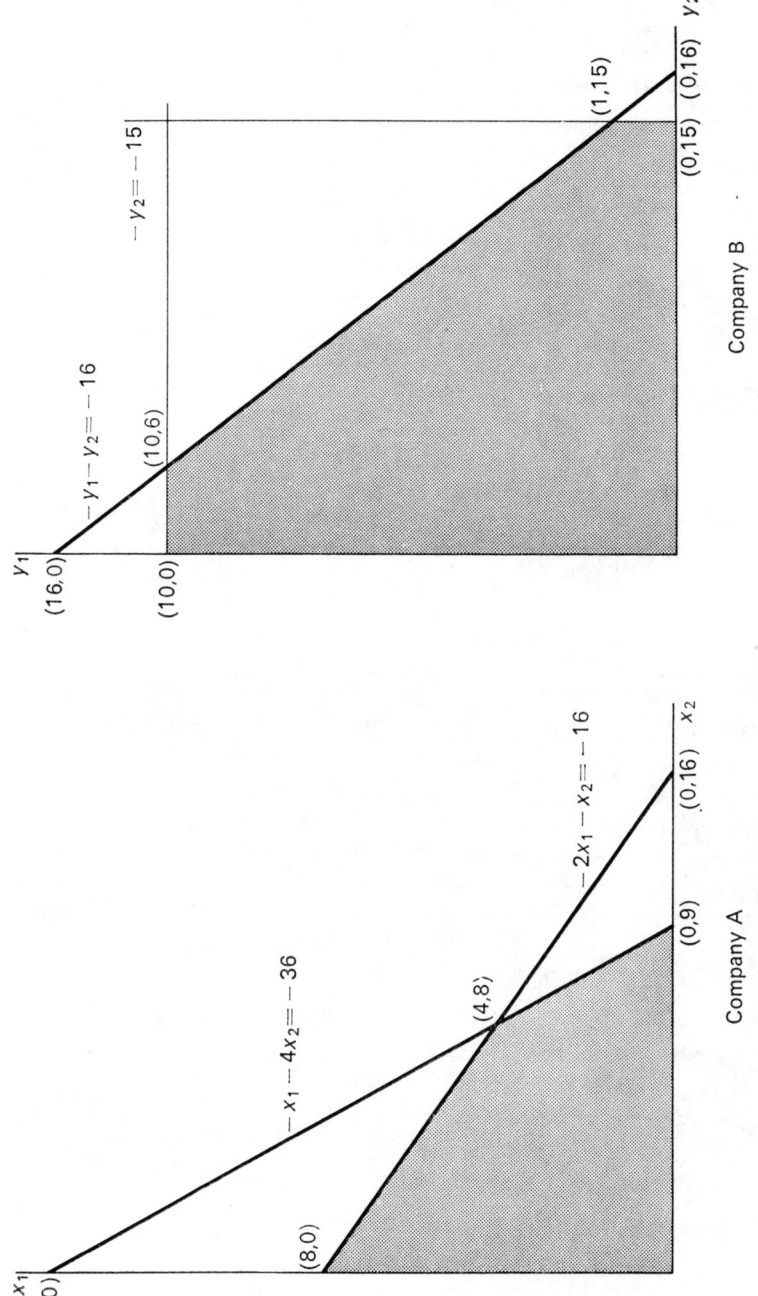

Fig. 4.2 Feasible regions for production in the two subsidiary companies.

TABLE 4.8
Successive problems in the decomposition algorithm

Subsidiary problem—company A Maximize $z_A \equiv 3x_1 + 3x_2$ Optimal solution: $(x_1{}^0, x_2{}^0) = (4, 8), z_A{}^0 = 36$	Subsidiary problem—company B Maximize $z_B \equiv 3y_1 + y_2$ Optimal solution: $(y_1{}^0, y_2{}^0) = (10, 6), z_B{}^0 = 36$

$$z_A{}^0 + z_B{}^0 = 72$$

1st master program

	x_1	x_2	y_1	y_2
λ_1	(4	8	10	6)
	+3	+3	+3	+1
	−1	−2	−2	−1

maximize $\quad 72\,\lambda_1$
subject to $\quad -46\,\lambda_1 \geqslant -40$
$\quad\quad\quad\quad -\ \lambda_1 \geqslant -1$

Simplex tableaux:

	λ_1	
s_1	(−46)	+40
s_2	−1	+1
	+72	

	s_1	
λ_1	$-\dfrac{1}{46}$	$\dfrac{40}{46}$
s_2	$\dfrac{1}{46}$	$\dfrac{6}{46}$
	$-\dfrac{72}{46}$	

Optimal solution:
$$\lambda_1{}^0 = \frac{40}{46},\ u_1{}^0 = \frac{72}{46},\ u_2{}^0 = 0$$

Subsidiary problem—company A Maximize $z_A \equiv \left(3 - \dfrac{72}{46}\right)x_1 + \left(3 - \dfrac{2 \cdot 72}{46}\right)x_2$ $\quad = +\dfrac{66}{46}x_1 - \dfrac{6}{46}x_2$ Optimal solution: $(x_1{}^0, x_2{}^0) = (8, 0), z_A{}^0 = \dfrac{528}{46}$	Subsidiary problem—company B Maximize $z_B \equiv \left(3 - \dfrac{2 \cdot 72}{46}\right)y_1 + \left(1 - \dfrac{72}{46}\right)y_2$ $\quad = -\dfrac{6}{46}y_1 - \dfrac{26}{46}y_2$ Optimal solution: $(y_1{}^0, y_2{}^0) = (0, 0), z_B{}^0 = 0$

$$z_A{}^0 + x_B{}^0 = \frac{528}{46}$$

2nd master program

	x_1	x_2	y_1	y_2
$+\lambda_2$	(8	0	0	0)
	+3	+3	+3	+1
	−1	−2	−2	−1

maximize $\quad 72\,\lambda_1 + 24\,\lambda_2$
subject to $\quad -46\,\lambda_1 -\ 8\lambda_2 \geqslant -40$
$\quad\quad\quad\quad -\lambda_1 -\ \lambda_2 \geqslant -1$

Simplex tableaux:

	λ_1	λ_2	
s_1	(−46)	−8	+40
s_2	−1	−1	+1
	+72	+24	

	s_1	λ_2	
λ_1	$-\dfrac{1}{46}$	$-\dfrac{8}{46}$	$\dfrac{40}{46}$
s_2	$\dfrac{1}{46}$	$\left(-\dfrac{38}{46}\right)$	$\dfrac{6}{46}$
	$-\dfrac{72}{46}$	$\dfrac{528}{46}$	

	s_1	s_2	
λ_1	$-\dfrac{1}{38}$	$\dfrac{8}{38}$	$\dfrac{32}{38}$
λ_2	$\dfrac{1}{38}$	$-\dfrac{46}{38}$	$\dfrac{6}{38}$
	$-\dfrac{48}{38}$	$\dfrac{528}{38}$	

Optimal solution:
$$\lambda_1{}^0 = \frac{32}{38},\ \lambda_2{}^0 = \frac{6}{38},\ u_1{}^0 = \frac{48}{38},\ u_2{}^0 = \frac{528}{38}$$

Computation and Valuation

TABLE 4.8 (*continued*)

Subsidiary problem—company A	Subsidiary problem—company B
Maximize $z_A \equiv \left(3 - \frac{48}{38}\right) x_1 + \left(3 - \frac{2 \cdot 48}{38}\right) x_2$	Maximize $z_B \equiv \left(3 - \frac{2 \cdot 48}{38}\right) y_1 + \left(1 - \frac{48}{38}\right) y_2$
$= \frac{66}{38} x_1 + \frac{18}{38} x_2$	$= \frac{18}{38} y_1 - \frac{10}{38} y_2$
Optimal solution:	Optimal solution:
$(x_1^\circ, x_2^\circ) = (4, 8), z_A{}^\circ = \frac{408}{38}$	$(y_1^\circ, y_2^\circ) = (10, 0), z_B{}^\circ = \frac{180}{38}$

$$z_A{}^\circ + z_B{}^\circ = \frac{588}{38}$$

3rd master program

	x_1	x_2	y_1	y_2
$+\lambda_3$	(4	8	10	0)
	+3	+3	+3	+1
	−1	−2	−2	−1

maximize $72 \lambda_1 + 24 \lambda_2 + 66 \lambda_3$
subject to $-46 \lambda_1 - 8 \lambda_2 - 40 \lambda_3 \geq -40$
$-\lambda_1 - \lambda_2 - \lambda_3 \geq -1$

Simplex tableaux:

	λ_1	λ_2	λ_3	
s_1	(−46)	−8	−40	+40
s_2	−1	−1	−1	+1
	72	24	66	

	s_1	λ_2	λ_3	
λ_1	$-\frac{1}{46}$	$-\frac{8}{46}$	$\frac{40}{46}$	$\frac{40}{46}$
s_2	$\frac{1}{46}$	$\left(-\frac{38}{46}\right)$	$-\frac{6}{46}$	$\frac{6}{46}$
	$-\frac{72}{46}$	$\frac{528}{46}$	$\frac{156}{46}$	

	s_1	s_2	λ_3	
λ_1	$-\frac{1}{38}$	$\frac{8}{38}$	$\left(\frac{32}{38}\right)$	$\frac{32}{38}$
λ_2	$\frac{1}{38}$	$-\frac{46}{38}$	$-\frac{6}{38}$	$\frac{6}{38}$
	$-\frac{48}{38}$	$-\frac{528}{38}$	$\frac{60}{38}$	

	s_1	s_2	λ_1	
λ_3	$-\frac{1}{32}$	$\frac{8}{32}$	$\frac{38}{32}$	1
λ_2	$\frac{1}{32}$	$-\frac{40}{52}$	$\frac{6}{32}$	0
	$-\frac{42}{32}$	$\frac{432}{32}$	$-\frac{60}{32}$	

Optimal solution:
$\lambda_1{}^\circ = \lambda_2{}^\circ = 0, \lambda_3{}^\circ = 1, u_1{}^\circ = \frac{43}{52}, u_2{}^\circ = \frac{432}{32}$

Subsidiary problem—company A	Subsidiary problem—company B
Maximize $z_A \equiv \left(3 - \frac{42}{32}\right) x_1 + \left(3 - \frac{2 \cdot 42}{32}\right) x_2$	Maximize $z_B \equiv \left(3 - \frac{84}{32}\right) y_1 + \left(1 - \frac{42}{32}\right) y_2$
$= \frac{54}{32} x_1 + \frac{12}{32} x_2$	$= \frac{12}{32} y_1 - \frac{10}{32} y_2$
Optimal solution:	Optimal solution:
$(x_1^\circ, x_2^\circ) = (4, 8), z_A{}^\circ = \frac{312}{32}$	$(y_1^\circ, y_2^\circ) = (10, 0), z_B{}^\circ = \frac{120}{32}$

$$z_A{}^\circ + z_B{}^\circ = \frac{432}{32}$$

shared facilities and the others define the series of, in this case two, subsidiary companies A and B. Company A operates two production activities A_1 and A_2 at levels x_1 and x_2, and company B operates activities B_1 and B_2 at levels y_1 and y_2. The feasible regions for the two companies are drawn out in Fig. 4.2. The aim of the exercise is to maximize total revenue of the firm as a whole.

The algorithm used here is based on a decomposition principle suggested by G. B. Dantzig and P. Wolfe in 1960. It considers that the parent company sets an internal charge for whatever facilities are shared between the subsidiaries. The onus is then on the subsidiaries to review a number of proposals about the way they might operate. Each time they maximize their own contribution to total revenue with some adjustment included for the cost of the shared facility. The parent company then constructs a *master program* in which it examines all these proposals and selects the extent to which they are taken up in the light of the availability of the shared facilities. As a result, another set of internal charges are computed from the valuations placed on the facilities, and these are then put to the subsidiaries for the process to be repeated.

In the example it is possible to start by considering a plentiful supply of facility C_1 which the parent company is prepared to give to the subsidiaries at no charge. Each subsidiary can then aim to maximize revenue without considering any restriction on the total quantity of facility C_1. From Fig. 4.2 the two subsidiaries together will propose a combined position $(x_1, x_2, y_1, y_2) = (4, 8, 10, 6)$. The problem is that then 46 units of facility will be required and a master program must be constructed to consider how this single proposal can be operated against the only alternative, zero production. To do this, it is considered that the first proposal is taken to an extent λ_1, $\lambda_1 \geqslant 0$, and, to maintain feasibility for the separate companies $\lambda_1 \leqslant 1$. The original objective function and constraints on the availability of the shared facility are then expressed entirely in terms of λ_1. This is shown in the first problem of Table 4.8 where the coefficients of λ_1 are derived entirely from the cross-products of the activity levels for the first production position and their coefficients in the activity table. The optimal solution to the problem provides, for the value of λ_1, $\lambda_1{}^0 = 40/46$, and the valuation on the shared facility is $u_i{}^0 = 72/46$. That for the employment of this first proposal is $u_2{}^0 = 0$. In other words, the proposal cannot be fully adopted because of the restriction on the facility C_1. This should therefore have a positive scarcity value instead of its original price of zero. In addition, the revenue level is increased by inclusion of the proposal instead of otherwise choosing to produce nothing, and so the production mix (4, 8, 10, 6) will be placed on the proposal list.

Computation and Valuation

The second stage involves asking the subsidiary companies to review their positions with the possible charge of 72/46 made for unit consumption of facility C_1. Maximizing net revenue for each of the companies A and B gives a new combined production proposal $(x_1, x_2, y_1, y_2) = (8, 0, 0, 0)$ for which net revenue is 528/46 after the new internal charges have been taken into account. The master program will now consider combining the earlier proposal with this new one in proportions λ_1 and λ_2 where, to keep the solutions within the feasible region, $\lambda_1 + \lambda_2 \leq 1$. In fact, the best combination of these two proposals leads to a situation where the value of the shared facility is 48/38, less than its internal price which was 72/46. The assessed value of the current proposals is 528/38, however, and, if the new price of 48/38 is presented to the subsidiary companies, their total net revenue becomes

$$\frac{408}{38} + \frac{180}{38} = \frac{588}{38}$$

which again shows an improvement.

When this third internal price, 48/38, is presented to the subsidiaries it leads to a master program where a third production proposal (4, 8, 10, 0) is created. Solving the optimization problem leads to a new charge for facility C_1 of 42/32 and an assessed marginal revenue value of 432/32 for the current proposals. When this latest price is put to the subsidiaries the last proposal is reiterated and the total net revenue is 432/32. The profitability of this proposal is as great as any currently considered and, because all sides will be satisfied with the price of the common facility, the algorithm is brought to a close. It turns out the last master program suggests that the production levels should be kept at $(x_1, x_2, y_1, y_2) = (4, 8, 10, 0)$ which just uses all the allocation of facility C_1.

The process of decomposition allows a partial decentralization of management of the whole firm. Two cases can arise in the final solution. In the first, as has occurred above, the optimal solution to the whole problem is also a basic solution to each of the individual subsidiary problems. It is possible, therefore, for the central firm to set prices and leave the separate companies to optimize some objective function of their own. Then the decision-making process would be fully decentralized. In the second case, which could well happen in problems with the above structure, the overall solution might involve a set of production levels which do not simultaneously provide basic feasible solution for the subsidiaries. In this situation it is quite possible that the overall optimum lies inside the feasible region of one of the companies and, as optimization problems are solved by boundary points, no set of prices exists that will persuade the firm to adopt the required selection of activities. Then, although the decomposition principle can be used to indicate a set of profitable proposals, the ultimate decision on the production mix has to be taken centrally. The lesson to be learnt is that not all the economic systems can be broken down by means of a pricing system.

5 Behaviour of the Firm

The previous two chapters have considered short-run aspects of production planning. Whether the immediate problem was minimizing cost of production with fixed output targets or maximization of net revenue with fixed levels of input, the approach was inward-looking, concerned with internal organization of activities. In the longer term, the firm is forced to be more conscious of its customers, suppliers and competitors and to be prepared to take investment decisions to improve its position. The emphasis therefore shifts from the determination of an optimal production plan to the reaction of management. The move is across the frontier from operational research to economics and the question now is not 'what is the best plan in specific circumstances?' but instead 'how does the firm react in different market situations?'.

5.1 Economic Models of the Firm

The traditional economic approach to the firm has been to assume that there is an entrepreneur who takes decisions solely on the basis of maximizing total profit. This certainly justifies the popularity of the revenue-maximizing exercises of the last chapter. In fact, the definition of 'profit' can be broadened to encompass all financial outgoings from and income to a firm including expenditure on capital goods such as machinery, transport fleets and factory buildings, rather than simply the goods used up in production. Then the principle is able to cope well with standard selling situations and provides a rationale for deciding how much and at what price output can be marketed.

Two extreme cases are *pure competition* and *monopoly*. In the first of these, the firm faces its customers along with a large number of competitors, so large that the output of any individual firm is swamped in terms of quantity. It is then not possible for it to affect the current market price by varying the amount it offers for sale and thus create a shortage or a glut of the product. The decision made by the firm will be confined to the amount that is output and the criteria will be the profitability of production at the going price. By contrast, in the second case, there is only one firm in the market and it has complete control over the market price. It will have to decide, by judging the reaction of its customers, what price to set and what quantity will then be sold. The decision this time is about the combination of price and quantity of output.

Broadly speaking, the detail of the mechanism for setting price and quantity depends on the character of the market itself. If it is operating *perfectly*, then the goods bought and sold will be clearly defined with no variation in packaging or quality, and all customers will know what prices are being offered by all the firms. It is usual to add some further properties of business behaviour, that 'unprofitable' or 'inefficient' firms either collapse because their shareholders lose confidence in their investments or are simply pushed out of the market by competitors, and that there is no difficulty for new firms to enter or leave the market. To all intents and purposes, perfect operation sets the scene for pure competition, and it is generally accepted that *perfect competition* is equivalent to pure competition. On the other hand, the above aspects of business behaviour are often dropped thus allowing monopolies or price-rings to be formed. Such situations are usually included under the heading *imperfect competition*, which generally covers the operation of markets that are not perfect.

In either perfect competition or the particular case of imperfect competition which allows a monopoly to form, there will be one price for each good. If under perfect competition there were two firms selling at different prices, then either the higher priced would be making a profit or be inefficient, or the lower priced firm would be making a loss. In the first of these, with cheaper goods available, customers would be expected to shift to the lower price. In the second, the firm would go bankrupt. If both happened there would be room for a third business to strike an intermediate price, attract custom and stay in business. Whichever possibility occurred, there would still be a single price. Alternatively, under imperfect competition with a monopoly ruling the market, there will only be one price anyway.

There are other features of imperfect markets that encourage price differentials. They are the use of brand-names to differentiate between goods, the emphasis on quality in explaining higher prices and the lack of widespread knowledge about particular prices. It is difficult to cope with these in the current framework and the tendency is to attempt to interpret them as variations on single-price situations.

When it comes to bargains struck in the market, the actual value of price and quantity can be determined in principle from the type of demand and supply curves discussed earlier. When the quantities demanded by all consumers at a particular price are aggregated they form a demand curve which will cross the similarly aggregated supply curve (see Fig. 5.1). Obviously, at the intersection quantity demanded

Behaviour of the Firm

equals that supplied, and the market would be in equilibrium. This could be *stable* and, once obtained, continue to exist, or *unstable* and quickly break down if ever the point is reached. The co-ordinates of the intersection provide a single market price and total quantity produced or consumed.

Unfortunately, there is a well-recognized gap between the established bases derived from economic theory and the observed behaviour of firms. One reason for this is that the situation in which firms are usually

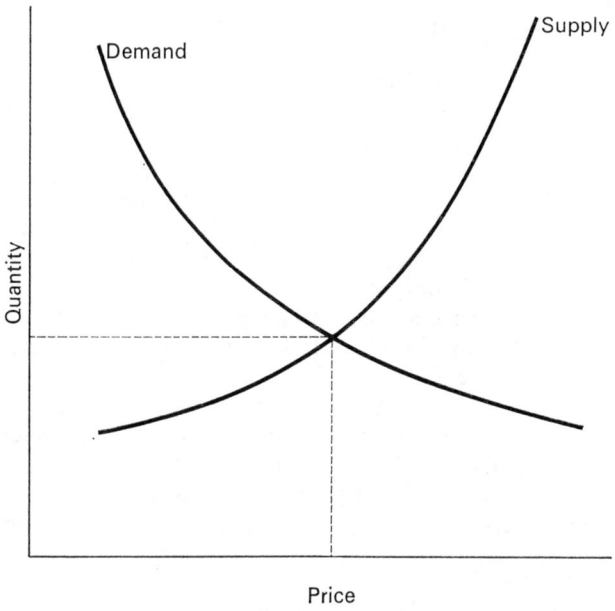

Fig. 5.1 The demand and supply curves intersecting at an equilibrium point.

placed falls between the two extremes of pure competition and monopoly. It is more like *monopolistic competition* where a number of firms have some control over the market price either through the large amounts that are output (the particular case of *oligopoly*) or by exploiting the imperfections of the market place, e.g. by creating a brand-image and thus setting up a monopoly in their own goods. Then there are more opportunities for direct conflict of interest between competitors, and the behaviour will be framed around the particular imperfections that protect their position. Some examples are the reinforcement of a brand-image, the spread of information that can be achieved by advertising, and the development of business strategies.

Also, as many production processes need at least a minimum level before they are viable commercially, there is more opportunity for the protection of markets against intrusion from possible competitors and innovation from technical developments.

So, the hypotheses about behaviour can be developed considerably beyond the original optimization of profit. The simple principle of optimization will however still be used to establish some important ideas through the two extremes of perfect competition and monopoly.

5.2 Perfect Competition

For a firm operating under perfect competition the dominant feature will be that the selling prices of its products are fixed. Equally, if it buys its supplies under perfect competition, the same condition will apply to prices of the inputs. Therefore, a firm that wishes to maximize profit would be expected in the short term to adjust its production position to the optimum described in the last chapter, the maximum net revenue. In the longer term the same principle would apply but with a more general interpretation.

When the aim was to solve a specific production problem the time horizon was determined at the outset. Now that it is required to model the firm's management decisions it is difficult to know whether to look at long or short term optimization. This must be decided so that the activity analysis framework can be drawn up. It makes a difference to the values chosen for coefficients in the activity table. For example, in the short term it would not be possible to introduce substantial changes in production methods because of the obvious lags in changing skills in the labour employed and re-equipping the workshop with new machines, whereas, in the long term, these changes could be made and the extra activities included in the table. Thus it is quite possible that a firm seeking a short-term optimum could work to a program that is not optimal in the long term. Also, because of the nature of the changes in methods, the reverse could be true.

Suppose initially that the technology of the firm is fixed and hence the coefficients in the activity table are the same in the short and long term. The production planning problem will therefore be the choice of activity levels x_j, $j = 1, \ldots n$ to maximize net revenue $\sum_{i=1}^{m} p_i x_{n+i}$ subject to the constraints

$$x_{n+i} = \sum_{j=1}^{n} a_{ij} x_j + b_i \geqslant 0, i = 1, \ldots m$$

$$x_j \geqslant 0, j = 1, \ldots n$$

The advice that comes from the optimal solution is framed in terms of imputed values u_i^0 of the goods and net imputed values $(p_i + u_i^0)$ of the allocations associated with each row constraint in the problem. In the last chapter, it was shown how they indicate the way in which constraints on the levels of production processes, the quantities of input supplied and the quantities of outputs produced can be altered to improve the profit situation.

To take up the example of the chemical firm for the optimum derived in Table 4.3, the most obvious candidates for adjustment are the quantities supplied of the chemicals C_2 and C_3 for which, when all costs are taken into account, the net values are -4 and $1 \cdot 5 - 2 = -0 \cdot 5$. Beyond the short term, action would be expected to 'balance up' production by reducing supply. This would be quite important for, when it was last considered, the firm was making a large loss of £12750. To see what it can now achieve, three tableaux are shown in Table 5.1 and illustrate some more profitable positions. They can be reached by reducing the supply of chemical C_2. In the first case, the drop is by an amount 2501 units which is slightly more than the spare chemical left over in the optimum of the last chapter. It brings production to a new position where chemical C_3 has a valuable role, making a net unit contribution of $2 \cdot 29 - 2 = 0 \cdot 29$ to revenue, while the actual value of chemical C_2 is still low compared with its price. By a reduction to a total supply of 10 999, activity A_4, which converts chemical C_2 into C_3, closes down and production is confined to activities A_1, A_2 and A_3. When the supply of C_2 reaches 9999, though, activity A_2 also ceases to be operative being no longer profitable even when there is an abundance of chemical C_3. Eventually, further drops in the quantities of chemicals C_2 and C_3 would leave the only profitable activity, A_1, operative. This would be when supplies are set at quantities 8000 and 4000 and profit has reached its highest level given the fixed capacity of the plant, viz. a value of £4000. Thus, the changes in supplies have brought the firm from its initial loss to a modest profit where both profitable and non-profitable activities were operating. Finally, by concentrating on the most efficient process, the greatest profit is achieved.

Once net revenue has reached some positive value, then it is possible to increase profit by changes in the overall scale of production. Because the technology is described by a system of linear equations, proportional changes that are simultaneously applied to the constants b_i on the right-hand sides of the constraints will lead to the same proportional changes in the quantities produced and profit achieved. The effect is to discard the stipulations where $b_i > 0$ which referred to fixed supplies and maximum plant size and which, in the long term, are restrictions that no longer apply. It is assumed that by multiplication

TABLE 5.1 **Effect of reducing supply of chemical C_2 to chemical firm**

Optimal tableau for supply of 12 499 units chemical C_2:

	x_9	x_8	x_{10}	x_7	
x_5					$+12\,499$
x_6					$+6\,000$
x_{11}	-0.83	0.16	-0.83	0.33	$+0.33$
x_2	0.83	-0.16	0.83	-0.33	$+999.66$
x_1	-1				$+4\,000$
x_3			-1		$+1\,000$
x_4	0.33	0.33	0.33	-0.33	$+499.66$
x_{12}	-0.33	-0.33	-0.33	0.33	$+4\,500.33$
	-5.5	-2.29	-3.5	-1.58	$-2\,744$

Optimal tableau for supply of 10 999 units chemical C_2:

	x_9	x_4	x_{10}	x_7	
x_5					$+10\,999$
x_6					$+6\,000$
x_{11}	-1	0.5	-1	0.5	$+500.5$
x_2	1	-0.5	1	-0.5	$+499.5$
x_1	-1				$+4\,000$
x_3			-1		$+1\,000$
x_8	-1	3	-1	1	$+1$
x_{12}				-1	$+5\,000$
	-3.25	-6.88	-1.25	-3.88	$+875$

Behaviour of the Firm

TABLE 5.1 (*contd.*)

Optimal tableau for supply of 9 999 units chemical C_2:

	x_9	x_4	x_2	x_7	
x_5					+9 999
x_6					+6 000
x_{11}			−1		+1 000
x_{10}	−1	0·5	1	0·5	+0·5
x_1	−1				+4 000
x_3	1	−0·5	−1	−0·5	+999·5
x_8		2·5	−1	0·5	+1 000·5
x_{12}		−1			+5 000
	−2	−7·5	−1·25	−4·5	+1 000

of present equipment, any level of production can be achieved. As a result, the description of the technology of production is left with just the relationships between quantities of goods and activity levels, the constraints on their signs and the stipulations for which $b_i = 0$. Thus the firm must choose a production position for which

$$x_{n+i} = \sum_{j=1}^{n} a_{ij} x_j \geqslant 0, \ i = 1, \ldots m$$

$$x_j \geqslant 0, \ j = 1, \ldots n$$

and take into account the resulting profit, $\sum_{i=1}^{m} p_i x_{n+i}$.

The set of relationships can be referred to as *first-order homogenous equations* because all terms have the variables x raised to power one. A percentage increase in all the variables will lead to the same increase in output. This is an important property and is quite often observed in the study of manufacturing industries when, in the long term, levels of labour and capital equipment are varied.

The direct result of removing the constraints is to create a difficulty. For the chemical firm, say, once it reaches any positive profit it could increase its value indefinitely by simply expanding production. This would seem to lead to the conclusion that a profit-maximizing firm will never reach an equilibrium, an unsatisfactory result for an explanatory model which, as yet, has no element of time. Therefore the framework must be re-examined. To reconcile the apparently unending profit stream it is necessary to look at the effect in the long run on the consumer. When faced with an increasing amount of the products he is only going to agree to absorb more than a given quantity if prices are dropped. This will take away some of the profit and, if the move continues, there will be a point where profit becomes zero, i.e. where there is no excess of outgoings over income. Of all the firms in the industry those who place the most reliance on efficient production activities will be prepared to suffer the greatest fall in prices. The others will either have the choice of selecting more profitable methods of production, or otherwise going out of business. Even if a combination of activities that just makes a profit is chosen at first, the firm will be forced to fit into the most efficient production pattern as defined at current prices. Once profit becomes zero, all expansion stops and the market assumes an equilibrium position.

This leads to an interesting situation, for, as all competing firms rely on the same production methods, the whole industry will have the same activity framework as the single firm. Therefore the original perfectly competitive market situation, where the quantity produced had no effect on prices, is lost. Instead there is a problem of general equilibrium of a sector of the economy with consumers and suppliers both reacting to the common price–quantity decisions of the firms. This is a topic discussed in chapter 9 but, for the present, it will be sufficient to remark that the overall equilibrium effectively creates further relationships between quantities input and output. For example, the availability of some resources and the demand for some products will be fixed in total over the industry. Because individual firms are simply scaled-down replicas of the industry this would mean a proportional relationship between the quantities of goods. In addition, there are other long-term constraints on, for example, the proportion of labour employed of different ages and skills, and relationships between, say, the amount of regular time and overtime worked. Therefore, the parts of the short-term production framework that remain can be enhanced by longer term restrictions on the proportionality between variable values.

Although it will now be understood what the long-term equilibrium looks like, it still is not known what are the values of the quantities and prices. The key lies in the production technology of the firm. It is known that the prices must be such that maximum profit for each firm is zero and, moreover, the profitability of any process used must also be zero. This does not necessarily tie down the values completely but at least provides a starting point. So, given an initial short-term production planning problem with a set of prices, it will be possible to select its most efficient activities, those that once the short-term stipulations

Behaviour of the Firm

have been discarded, give the greatest profit per unit of operation. It will be shown that, if these are the activities which remain in the long-term equilibrium, prices that would be expected to give the zero profit can be derived from the imputed valuations that result from suitable optimization problems.

For the chemical firm example the long-term technology could be described by Table 5.2. Two sets of prices are given, the first leaves a

TABLE 5.2

The long-term technology of the chemical firm

Goods		Activities				Stipula-tions	Prices X	Prices Y
		A_1 $x_1 \geqslant 0$	A_2 $x_2 \geqslant 0$	A_3 $x_3 \geqslant 0$	A_4 $x_4 \geqslant 0$			
Sales chemical C_1	$x_5 =$	3	2	3		$\geqslant 0$	4	5
Bought chemical C_2	$x_6 =$	2	2	2	1	$\geqslant 0$	−4	−3
Bought chemical C_3	$x_7 =$	1	2	1	−2	$\geqslant 0$	−3	−6
Used plant P_1 regular	$x_8 =$	1				$\geqslant 0$		
Used plant P_1 overtime	$x_9 =$			1		$\geqslant 0$		
Used plant P_2	$x_{10} =$		1			$\geqslant 0$		
Used plant P_3	$x_{11} =$				1	$\geqslant 0$		
Direct cost	$x_{12} =$	1	0·25	3	3	$\geqslant 0$	−1	−3
Net revenue X		0	−6·25	−2	−1			
Net revenue Y		0	−8·75	−6	0			

zero profit for activity A_1 and negative profit for the rest, and the second gives a zero profit to both activities A_1 and A_4. Clearly, if a particular activity A_j is operable in the long-term equilibrium, the prices of the goods must be such that

$$\sum_{i=1}^{m} p_i a_{ij} = 0$$

For all other goods,

$$\sum_{i=1}^{m} p_i a_{ij} \leqslant 0$$

In the example, both sets of prices could apply in a long-term equilibrium, as could a large number of others. The question here is how at least one set of prices can be found using the imputed values. For the example it was a simple matter of inspection, but this need not be so generally.

To form the necessary optimization problem, consider that it is required to maximize the revenue obtained from a unit level of operation of the firm as a whole. Let the unit be defined by a linear combination of quantities of goods, $\sum_{i=1}^{m} a_i x_{n+i}$ (where a sufficient number of values a_i are positive to be meaningful), which, to ease notation, can be written in terms of the activity levels, say, $-\sum_{j=1}^{n} a_{0j} x_j$. Then it will be required to maximize net revenue,

$$\sum_{i=1}^{m} p_i x_{n+i} = \sum_{i=0}^{m} \sum_{j=1}^{n} p_i a_{ij} x_j$$

subject to the constraints

$$\sum_{j=1}^{n} a_{0j} x_j + 1 \geqslant 0$$

$$x_{n+i} = \sum_{j=1}^{n} a_{ij} x_j \geqslant 0, i = 1, \ldots m$$

while $x_j \geqslant 0, j = 1, \ldots n$, and where $p_0 = 0$.

The Kuhn–Tucker conditions state that, for some set u_i^0, $i = 0, \ldots m$ and for the optimum x_j^0, the following relationships hold

$$-\sum_{i=0}^{m} p_i a_{ij} - \sum_{i=0}^{m} a_{ij} u_i^0 \geqslant 0, j = 1, \ldots n$$

i.e.

$$\sum_{i=0}^{m} (p_i + u_i^0) a_{ij} \leqslant 0, j = 1, \ldots n$$

where $u_i^0 \geqslant 0$, and also

$$\sum_{i=0}^{m} \sum_{j=1}^{n} (p_i + u_i^0) a_{ij} x_j^0 = 0$$

Behaviour of the Firm

As when they were used before, the conditions provide a concise way of expressing what has been derived intuitively. They help create a system of valuation for the goods produced and consumed which has the following properties:

$$u_i^0 > 0 \text{ implies } x_{n+i}^0 = \sum_{j=1}^{n} a_{ij} x_j^0 = 0$$

and

$$x_{n+i}^0 > 0 \text{ implies } u_i^0 = 0$$

for $i = 1, \ldots m$. These conditions are already familiar from the discussions of valuations of the goods in the last chapter. In fact, the set of values u_i^0 are the imputed valuations of the goods in this problem.

If a new variable is defined $q_i = u_i + p_i, i = 0, \ldots m$, the conditions can be restated so that, at the optimum,

$$\sum_{i=0}^{m} q_i^0 a_{ij} \leqslant 0, j = 1, \ldots n$$

$$q_i^0 \geqslant p_i, i = 0, \ldots m$$

The solution also satisfies

$$\sum_{i=0}^{m} \sum_{j=1}^{n} q_i^0 a_{ij} x_j^0 = 0$$

and hence

$$x_j^0 > 0 \text{ implies } \sum_{i=0}^{m} q_i^0 a_{ij} = 0$$

and

$$\sum_{i=0}^{m} q_i^0 a_{ij} < 0 \text{ implies } x_j^0 = 0$$

The set q_i^0, $i = 1, \ldots m$, provides prices for the goods which, together with additional unit costs placed on the activities A_j at rates $-a_{0j} q_0^0$, ensure that any production activity that operates does so at zero profit. The unit costs can be amalgamated into the prices to give a final figure of $(q_i^0 + a_i q_0^0)$ where the previous profit is dispersed over the prices of the goods. Therefore these are the prices at which profit-maximizing firms would be satisfied in a long-term equilibrium.

To see what this derivation of prices would give for the example, suppose that the level of operation of the firm is to be judged by the total output of chemical C_1, i.e. by the size of variable x_5. By substituting from the activity table, this becomes $(3x_1 + 2x_2 + 3x_3)$. The first constraint of the optimization problem therefore becomes

$$-3x_1 - 2x_2 - 3x_3 + 1 \geqslant 0$$

and can be set alongside the eight constraints of Table 5.2. Also, to derive the objective function for the problem, suppose that currently the prices of goods are those used in the last chapter, namely £4 for sales C_1, £(-4) for bought C_2, £(-2) for bought C_3 and £(-1) for each unit of direct cost. The function that is to be maximized will therefore be $(x_1 - 4 \cdot 25x_2 - x_3 - 3x_4)$. By inspection, its optimal value can be seen to be attained when $x_1^0 = 0 \cdot 33$, $x_2^0 = x_3^0 = x_4^0 = 0$. Therefore, from the specification of the technology, $x_5^0 = 1$, $x_6^0 = 0 \cdot 67$, $x_7^0 = x_8^0 = x_{12}^0 = 0 \cdot 33$ and $x_9^0 = x_{10}^0 = x_{11}^0 = 0$. If multipliers u_i^0 are attached to the rows associated with variables x_{n+i}, where $n = 4$ and $i = 1, \ldots 8$, in Table 5·2, and u_0^0 with the above constraint on the level of operation of the firm as a whole, then the values that satisfy the Kuhn–Tucker conditions can be derived according to the occurrence of positive values for the variables. As x_5^0, x_6^0, x_7^0, x_8^0, $x_{12}^0 > 0$, then $u_1^0 = u_2^0 = u_3^0 = u_4^0 = u_8^0 = 0$. In addition, because $x_1^0 = 0 \cdot 33 > 0$, it follows that

$$1 - 3u_0^0 + 3u_1^0 + 2u_2^0 + u_3^0 + u_4^0 + u_8^0 = 0$$

i.e.

$$u_0^0 = 0 \cdot 33$$

while the remaining multiplier values, u_5^0, u_6^0 and u_7^0 can be chosen at any non-negative levels that satisfy simultaneously

$$-4 \cdot 25 - 2u_0^0 + 2u_1^0 + 2u_2^0 + 2u_3^0 + u_6^0 + 0 \cdot 25u_8^0 \leqslant 0$$
$$-1 \quad - 3u_0^0 + 3u_1^0 + 2u_2^0 + \; u_3^0 + u_5^0 + \quad 3u_8^0 \leqslant 0$$

and

$$-3 \qquad\qquad\qquad + u_2^0 - u_3^0 + u_7^0 + \quad 3u_8^0 \leqslant 0$$

i.e. $u_6^0 \leqslant 4 \cdot 92$, $u_5^0 \leqslant 2$, and $u_7^0 \leqslant 3$.

If these three multipliers are set equal to zero, then the summary of modifications to the original prices will be as follows:

$$u_1^0 + a_i q_0^0 = -0 \cdot 33$$
$$u_i^0 + a_i q_0^0 = 0, i = 2, 3, \ldots 8$$

Hence the long-term equilibrium prices derived will differ from the originals by a reduction only in the price of chemical C_1 of £0.33. As

Behaviour of the Firm

a result, activity A_1 can operate using plant P_1 on regular time at zero profit whilst the other activities would make a negative profit. Alternatively, if the choice were made that $u_6^0 = 4.92$, $u_5^0 = 2$ and $u_7^0 = 3$, then, besides the lower price for chemical C_1 there would have to be additional subsidies made for the use of plant P_1 on overtime, plant P_2 and plant P_3. The size of these subsidies would be £4.92, £2 and £3 respectively and, if made, would ensure that all plants could be used at zero profitability in the long-term equilibrium.

5.3 Non-linearities; Variable Returns to Scale and Monopolies

The Kuhn-Tucker conditions allow a general extension of the principle of imputed values to models of production that contain non-linearities in the production coefficients and objective function. This is useful for it enables the above discussions to be carried over to situations where there are non-constant returns to scale and where one firm has a monopolistic hold over the markets in which it buys and sells goods.

In the first case, the linear constraint equations are replaced by non-linear functions that describe the economies or diseconomies which an increase in scale of operation brings. Some examples are the advantages of pooling manpower, facilities and resources in the areas of management, marketing, finance and research. Others are the disadvantages of greater complexity in management decisions and establishment of training facilities associated with large organizations. Profit remains a linear function, and the overall aim for each firm is still to achieve the largest profit possible. An organization would therefore be encouraged to expand in the first instance at least up to a point where the total profit ceases to increase. Looking at the industry, however, while some profit is being made, new firms would be encouraged to enter the market. Whether they do so or not depends on the strength of the economies and diseconomies for different levels of production. Invariably there will be a value for the optimal size of firm. If this is small, the industry will contain small firms which can easily leave or enter the market. Total changes in quantities of production will have an impact on the price at which the consumers want to buy, and eventually profit for each firm will be brought to zero. On the other hand, the optimal size of firm might be large in which case it could be difficult to enter or leave the market. In fact, at the extreme, if economies of scale was the dominant feature of the industry, then a monopolistic situation would be reached.

For the monopoly, consumer demand and the suppliers' own production choices will dictate the set of possible price-quantity combinations at which markets can operate. Thus, in the objective function, price will no longer be constant but will be a function of quantity.

Usually the actual relationship is derived by inverting the simple demand or supply curves which separately relate quantity to price for each good. When, though, there are strong interrelationships between the quantity decisions of different goods, this will not necessarily be straightforward and several industries might have to be included at the same time. Whatever the complexity, the result will be a model for a firm in a monopoly position where the mechanism relies on the maximization of a non-linear profit function subject to linear technology constraints.

Traditionally, a monopoly would be expected to expand up to a point where profit begins to level off, i.e. where the marginal profit is zero. It will then be content to hold the level of production, protected as it is from potential competitors entering the market. Hence there will be no zero profit equilibrium, and actual prices need not necessarily match the marginal valuations. Indeed the actual profit may be equal or less than zero and some prices less than the imputed values. Then, the firm can only remain in operation through subsidies from other firms who rely on the prestige of, say, goods produced under a tradename, or from a government which has its own reasons for maintaining the industry.

The non-linearities can be considered generally by taking a firm that chooses activity levels x_j, $j = 1, \ldots n$, to maximize profit, $f(x_1 \ldots x_n)$, subject to general technological constraints

$$g_i(x_1, \ldots x_n) \geqslant 0, i = 1, \ldots m$$

where

$$x_j \geqslant 0, j = 1, \ldots n$$

If the functions f and g_i are differentiable and demonstrate diminishing marginal returns in the trade-offs between changes in the activity levels, then it will be possible to make the assumption that they are concave and the feasible region is convex. The Kuhn–Tucker conditions imply that at the optimum, $x_1^0, \ldots x_n^0$, there exist a set of non-negative values u_i^0 which satisfy

$$\frac{\delta f}{\delta x_j} + \sum_{i=1}^{m} u_i^0 \frac{\delta g_i}{\delta x_j} \leqslant 0, j = 1, \ldots n$$

while

$$\sum_{j=1}^{n} \left(\frac{\delta f}{\delta x_j} + \sum_{i=1}^{m} u_i^0 \frac{\delta g_i}{\delta x_j} \right) x_j^0 = \sum_{i=1}^{m} g_i(x_1^0, \ldots x_n^0) u_i^0 = 0$$

This again provides a system of imputed values that correspond to the 'row' constraints $g_i \geqslant 0$. If any constraint is not met, i.e. $g_i > 0$, then

Behaviour of the Firm

the valuation on that aspect of production will be zero. Also if any good is present in a positive amount, $x_j^0 > 0$, then

$$\frac{\delta f}{\delta x_j} + \sum_{i=1}^{m} u_i^0 \frac{\delta g_i}{\delta x_j} = 0$$

i.e., the extra revenue derived from expanding the production activity plus the value of the resulting changes in constraint levels is zero. In broad terms this means that the marginal profit obtained from shifts in production is zero.

In the specific case of a firm operating under varying returns to scale the function f can be replaced by a linear expression. To draw a parallel to the completely linear problem, the remaining functions g_i can be rewritten

$$g_i \equiv \sum_{j=1}^{n} a_{ij} x_j$$

where the coefficients a_{ij} are themselves functions of activity levels x_j. By identifying the row constraints with goods whose prices p_i are fixed, the objective function can be expressed as

$$f \equiv \sum_{i=1}^{m} \sum_{j=1}^{n} a_{ij} p_i x_j = \sum_{i=1}^{m} p_i g_i$$

The conditions for maximum profit can then be written

$$\sum_{i=1}^{m} (p_i + u_i^0) \frac{\delta g_i}{\delta x_j} \leqslant 0, j = 1, \ldots n$$

where

$$\sum_{i=1}^{m} \sum_{j=1}^{n} (p_i + u_i^0) \frac{\delta g_i}{\delta x_j} x_j^0 = \sum_{i=1}^{m} \sum_{j=1}^{n} a_{ij} x_j^0 u_i^0 = 0$$

and u_i^0 are a set of non-negative values. There is a resemblance to the conditions for the linear problem, but the partial derivatives $\delta g_i/\delta x_j$ are not usually equal to the coefficients a_{ij} and it is not possible to use the last equation to set optimal profit equal to zero. In fact, profit is not necessarily zero at the given prices. A set of prices that would make it zero are the values u_i^0, i.e., the marginal revenues of the goods, and these will supply the prices for a possible long-term equilibrium position. When $x_j^0 > 0$, however, it will not necessarily be true that $\sum_{i=1}^{m} a_{ij} u_i^0 = 0$ for an activity A_j, and the zero profit position could include a balanced mixture of processes that give both positive and negative profits.

For the monopoly situation the prices p_i will be functions of the activity levels while the coefficients a_{ij} remain constant. The Kuhn–Tucker conditions then indicate that, at the optimal solution,

$$\sum_{i=1}^{m}\sum_{j=1}^{n}\frac{\delta p_i}{\delta x_k}a_{ij}x_j^0 + \sum_{i=1}^{m}(p_i+u_i^0)a_{ik} \leqslant 0, k=1,\ldots n$$

A simplified form for the partial derivatives $\delta p_i/\delta x_j$ is obtained when the demand curves are not interrelated, i.e. selling (or buying) price of a good is a function only of the quantity produced (or consumed) of that good, namely x_{n+i} where

$$x_{n+i} = \sum_{j=1}^{n} a_{ij}x_j$$

Thus,

$$\frac{\delta p_i}{\delta x_k} = \frac{dp_i}{dx_{n+i}}\frac{\delta x_{n+i}}{\delta x_k} = \frac{dp_i}{dx_{n+i}}a_{ik}, k=1,\ldots n$$

and the above conditions can be rephrased as

$$\sum_{i=1}^{m}\left(p_i+u_i^0+\frac{dp_i}{dx_{n+i}}\sum_{j=1}^{n}a_{ij}x_j^0\right)a_{ik} \leqslant 0, k=1,\ldots n$$

To complete the set of conditions, it is also true that

$$\sum_{i=1}^{m}\sum_{j=1}^{n}\left(p_i+u_i^0+\frac{dp_i}{dx_{n+i}}\sum_{j=1}^{n}a_{ij}x_j^0\right)a_{ik}x_k^0 = \sum_{i=1}^{m}\sum_{j=1}^{n}a_{ij}x_j^0u_i^0 = 0$$

The existence of the extra term

$$\frac{dp_i}{dx_{n+i}}\sum_{j=1}^{n}a_{ij}x_j^0$$

means that the actual profit is non-zero. Using the last equality line, profit,

$$\sum_{i=1}^{m}\sum_{j=1}^{n}p_i a_{ik}x_k^0 = -\sum_{i=1}^{n}\sum_{j=1}^{n}\sum_{k=1}^{n}\frac{dp_i}{dx_{n+i}}x_k^0 a_{ij}x_j^0$$

The term also represents the difference between the current prices and those that would give the same production position under perfect competition. In a sense, the values it takes are the distortions in prices brought about by the monopoly.

5.4 Market Games

Between the two extremes of perfect competition and monopoly lies monopolistic competition where a number of firms are able to influence market prices and compete with each other using all the

Behaviour of the Firm

methods at their disposal. It is disappointing that then economic theory cannot cope so adequately in describing the mechanisms of interaction. In some cases, it is possible to adapt the arguments of the previous sections. For example, one firm might dominate a market and leave whatever 'crusts' are left for other smaller firms to pick up. It would be expected to be able to dictate price levels and, if it took into account the responses of the other firms in the market, could behave as a simple monopoly. This powerful position would have to be maintained, though, by embarking on a price war, undercutting potential competitors and relying on the firm's superior financial standing to hold out while they face bankruptcy. Another example would be firms joining together in a consortium to fix selling price and act as one large monopoly. Broadly speaking, then, when there are two or more large firms in the market, the detailed behaviour has to be considered of both the customers and competitors.

A simple example of such a situation is two firms 1 and 2 competing for a fixed number of orders from customers. Suppose that there are 1000 orders, all of the same size, and that each customer is first approached by the two firms each offering one discount rate. This could be 5 or 7 per cent according to current policy. The customer then makes up his mind from whom he will buy. What one firm gains, the other loses, and the solution of the apparent conflict is described as a *constant-sum game*. The final outcome can be indicated by the *pay-off matrix* in Table 5.3 where entries in the matrix indicate the number of

TABLE 5.3
Pay-off matrix for the conflict between firms 1 and 2

		Discount strategy of firm 2		
		5%	7%	
Discount strategy of firm 1	5%	600	100	Minimum 100
	7%	800	400	Minimum 400
		Maximum 800	Maximum 400	

orders obtained by firm 1 when both firms operate their chosen discount rates. Their decisions will be the *strategies* which they adopt in the market game.

A likely strategy is one where an entrepreneur puts considerable emphasis on the possibility that he might come out of the conflict with a small number of orders. He would then judge the rates by looking at the smallest outcome from his point of view and choose the rate that gave him the highest lower limit. In other words, a cautious entrepreneur would be expected to choose the discount that gave him the largest minimum advantage or alternatively his competitor the smallest maximum advantage. This is known as the *maxi–min*, or *mini–max*, strategy and can be applied for firm 1 by noting the minimum values in the rows, 100 and 400. The maximum of these is 400 and so, if firm 1 chooses to offer a discount of 7 per cent, no matter what firm 2 does, firm 1 is guaranteed at least 400 orders. The maxi–min choice for firm 1 is a 7 per cent discount. Similarly, firm 2 would choose the discount that provides the largest minimum gain to himself, i.e. the smallest maximum gain to firm 1. The mini–max strategy for firm 2 means choosing 7 per cent also, and the final outcome will be 400 orders to firm 1 and 600 orders to firm 2. This coincides with what each firm calculated from its maxi–min and mini–max considerations and they would therefore be expected to be content with the outcome. Hence the market would be in an equilibrium if the exercise were repeated.

Unfortunately, these arguments cannot be extended generally. The games considered must have a constant-sums pay-off matrix, and the description of gains and losses does not allow development to situations where a large discount could attract, say, more orders in total. Nevertheless it is possible to apply the techniques to more complex situations where there are a large number of strategies and also where the outcomes are determined by probability distributions. An important extension is also the introduction of 'mixed strategies'.

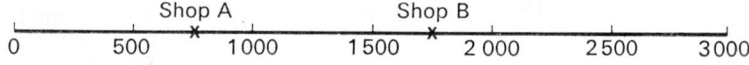

Fig. 5.2 Two shops, A and B, in a linear town.

If more strategies are included in the game it is possible to illustrate a classical problem in the location of business activities. Suppose two shops, A and B, can be located at any point on the only street of a long linear town where customers are expected to favour the nearest shop with their business (see Fig. 5.2). The question lies with where each shopowner will choose to site his premises. The pay-off matrix for

Behaviour of the Firm

TABLE 5.4

Pay-off matrix for shop A in its location in the linear town

		Location strategy of shop B							
		0	500	1 000	1 500	2 000	2 500	3 000	Minimum
Location strategy of shop A	0	1 500	250	500	1 750	1 000	1 250	1 500	250
	500	2 750	1 500	750	1 000	1 250	1 500	1 750	750
	1 000	2 500	2 250	1 500	1 250	1 500	1 750	2 000	1 250
	1 500	2 250	2 000	1 750	1 500	1 750	2 000	2 250	1 500
	2 000	2 000	1 750	1 500	1 250	1 500	2 250	2 500	1 250
	2 500	1 750	1 500	1 250	1 000	750	1 500	2 750	750
	3 000	1 500	1 250	1 000	750	500	250	1 500	250
Maximum		2 750	2 250	1 750	1 500	1 750	2 250	2 750	

shop A, in terms of 3000 customers, say, spread evenly through the town, is given in Table 5.4 where location is measured in yards from one end of the town. If the mini–max strategy is applied, it leads to both shops choosing to locate at the central point in the town. Once there, neither shop would wish to move for, if it did, it would then incur a smaller share of the trade. This solution is not a particularly good one from the community's point of view because the customers have to travel further than they need. The allocation by a central planning body attempting to minimize travel costs would lead to the shops being situated at 750 yards from each end. Then, they would still hold the same amount of trade but the customer's travelling expenses would be less. This is a classical situation used in arguments for central planning.

The two examples considered so far have led to an equilibrium solution where the actual outcome equalled what was expected from the maxi–min strategy of one firm and the mini–max strategy of the other. There are situations where this need not be so. For example, suppose when the two firms offer their discount rates they tie to them different delivery dates with the result that the reaction of the customers is different and the pay-off matrix is that of Table 5.5. If firm 1 follows a maxi–min strategy, it will choose the 5 per cent discount and expect 400 orders while firm 2 will choose the 5 per cent rate and expect 500 orders. What will actually happen is that firm 1 will gain an unexpected 500 orders and firm 2, although it also receives 500 orders, will be put in a position where it would be encouraged to shift to the 7 per cent rate and stand to gain an extra 100 orders thus pushing

TABLE 5.5

Modified pay-off matrix for the conflict between firms 1 and 2

		Discount strategy of firm 2		
		5%	7%	
Discount strategy of firm 1	5%	500	400	Minimum 400
	7%	300	600	Minimum 300
		Maximum 500	Maximum 600	Pay-off for firm 1

firm 1 to its maxi–min position. Equally, if firm 1 suspects such action from firm 2, it could retaliate by raising its own discount to 7 per cent and thus stand to gain orders. Both firms would be expected in future to behave unpredictably and no equilibrium is reached. It can be shown that it would be reached, though, if the final discount rate was chosen by a suitable chance selection, a *mixed strategy*. As long as the probabilities of the choice of a strategy are carefully controlled, there is no need for the actual decision to be determinable by the firm itself, let alone by its competitor, until the last minute.

Suppose that firm 1 chooses its discount rate by drawing lots so that the probability it chooses the 5 per cent rate is denoted by p_1 and the 7 per cent rate p_2. Of course, $p_1 + p_2 = 1$. The maxi–min strategy will require finding the probability values that ensure that, for each possible retaliatory move by the other firm, the *expected pay-off*, the sum of the pay-offs weighted by the probability values, exceeds as high a minimum standard as possible. In other words, the smallest of the expected pay-offs corresponding to each column must be as large as possible. In linear programming terms, it is required to maximize the minimum value r, i.e. maximize r, subject to

$$500p_1 + 300p_2 \geqslant r$$
$$400p_1 + 600p_2 \geqslant r$$
$$p_1 + p_2 = 1$$

Behaviour of the Firm

where p_1, p_2 and r are all variables. In this problem the expected pay-offs will be positive, as will the largest value of r. Therefore, by defining new variables

$$x_j = \frac{p_j}{r}, j = 1, 2,$$

it is possible to simplify the problem to give,

minimize $\quad \dfrac{1}{r} = x_1 + x_2$

subject to

$$500x_1 + 300x_2 \geqslant 1$$
$$400x_1 + 600x_2 \geqslant 1$$
$$x_1, x_2 \geqslant 0$$

In this case the optimal solution is $(x_1^0, x_2^0) = (1/600, 1/1800)$ and, using the formula

$$p_j = rx_j = \frac{x_j}{x_1 + x_2}, j = 1, 2,$$

implies that the optimal strategy is to choose the discount rates 5 and 7 per cent with probabilities $(p_1^0, p_2^0) = (\frac{3}{4}, \frac{1}{4})$. Thus the lowest expected pay-off for firm 1 will be the minimum of $(500.\frac{3}{4} + 300.\frac{1}{4})$ and $(400.\frac{3}{4} + 600.\frac{1}{4})$ which both equal 450. The use of probabilities to mix the strategies will raise firm 1's expectations from a definite 400 to an average 450 orders.

At the same time, if firm 2 decides to retaliate using a mixed strategy it would construct another problem derived from trying to maximize a ceiling, s, on the expectations of firm 1's gain when there were probabilities q_1 and q_2 placed on firm 2's choice of discount rates. This gives a linear programming problem of maximizing $1/s = y_1 + y_2$ subject to

$$500y_1 + 400y_2 \leqslant 1$$
$$300y_1 + 600y_2 \leqslant 1$$
$$y_1, y_2 \geqslant 0$$

where $y_i = q_i/s$, $i = 1, 2$, are variables defined similarly to the variables x_j. The optimal solution is $(y_1^0, y_2^0) = (1/900, 1/900)$ which implies in terms of the probabilities, $(q_1^0, q_2^0) = (\frac{1}{2}, \frac{1}{2})$. Firm 2 will place an equal probability on the two discount rates and will expect that 450 orders are lost to firm 1. As this coincides with the expectation of firm 1, the market would be in equilibrium.

These two linear programming problems illustrate the principle of duality, and their optimal solutions are related in a number of ways (see Appendix B). The feature of duality that is important here is the equality of the values of the solutions to the problems. It will always occur, and the application of mixed strategies will therefore generally provide equilibrium.

The introduction of the ideas of mini–max and mixed strategies adds an extra dimension to the modelling of conflict situations. The actual applications, though, are rare and it remains a difficult problem to represent the intricacies of manoeuvres in the usual market situations.

5.5 Alternative Objectives

Perhaps the most serious deficiency of the theories have been their dependence on the maximization of profit. A more realistic alternative is that sales revenue is maximized subject to the technology of production and the maintenance of profit above a given level. Another possibility is simply concentration on containing values of a number of criteria, such as sales revenue and profit, within given acceptable limits from one point in time to the next. No such assumption, though, has been as well accepted as profit-maximization nor has given such useful conclusions. So, before throwing it away, it would be advisable to consider how many results can be drawn from its replacement.

In other terms, the models lack consideration of the time element. They are static rather than dynamic. It would be expected that the entrepreneur attempts to achieve some objective, at least on the lines of profit, by given points in time. These could well be tied to meetings of directors or shareholders, applications to banks for loans or simply the end of the tax year. Further, as time progresses, research efforts could help improve the production technology, and the market prices change in response to consumers shifting their tastes and preferences. The respective effects of these two possibilities is to introduce a time parameter into the coefficients a_{ij} and the objective function prices p_i. A still further possibility is that the uncertainty about these values for an entrepreneur attempting to forecast forward would be better expressed by using probability distributions. The result of introducing time, then, is to increase greatly the size of the problem through the extra detail that has to be included. For the present the dynamic aspects have been left out, but some further mention will be made in chapter 10.

6 Transport Planning

When considering the operation of a firm, it was necessary to include in the 'production process' everything that happens between taking charge of the 'inputs' and disposing of the 'outputs'. One item that usually makes its presence felt on the cost side of balance sheets is transport. It is as much a part of production as any other and, according to the responsibility of the firm and the location of its premises, will involve collection of materials from suppliers, transfer of components from one factory to another, distribution of the finished product to warehouses and delivery to customers. Until now the cost of these activities was hidden in the 'direct costs' evaluated in the activity table, and in the prices quoted for supplies and products. This does not necessarily provide an adequate basis for either decision-making or for a description of behaviour under competition. The figures that have been used in the last two chapters were supposedly calculated for delivery, say, to the factory gate or at least to some standard distribution depot. The costs for delivery away from that gate or depot would be expected to be generally higher, and to be spread out according to distances on a surface of costs. Therefore, it would be more appropriate to relate the policy of charging for transport to this pattern of costs either for decisions about prices presented to actual suppliers or customers, or for assessment of the 'direct costs' in a deeper analysis of production activities.

For convenience of organization, a firm's transport operations could be expected to be centralized in a single department and the directive given 'to cater for the needs of the whole firm as efficiently as possible'. In terms of the criteria of previous chapters this could be rephrased as attempting to maximize profit. In the short term, it will require minimizing the cost of delivering specific quantities to specific points, while, for the long term, indicating the shortcomings of current facilities in the context of the whole firm's transport needs. This raises the issue of what adjustments can be made within the scope of present facilities and how these facilities should be modified in the future.

In a more general sense, the organization of firms' transport plays a part in the economics of competition. Geographical patterns develop for prices of goods and rents of land as firms seek to locate themselves advantageously with respect to access to suppliers and customers. This, after all, is one of the prime reasons for the existence of the present cities, towns and industrial areas. What is particularly important is that, in practice, one of the few ways in which a firm can take a lead over its competitors is by exploiting location. Its technology, quality of output, skills of employees and credit-worthiness will usually be little different from its rival, and, apart from individual aptitudes of management and its past programme of capital investment, some of the only advantages it can gain are in terms of transport costs. In other words, for many firms the efficiency of transport operations may well spell out the 'make-or-break' point with respect to its competitors. When transport costs are high, it is in its interests to concentrate the search on finding a small percentage improvement on the transport side.

It is not only in the private sector that transportation is of considerable importance. A large amount of time and effort is spent in urban areas, say, travelling to and from work. If it were turned into production, this would add noticeably to the area's daily productive capacity. An incentive is therefore given to the urban transport planner to examine the provision of transport services for commuting, and also for all other daily travel needs. The same type of questions will occur to him as to the entrepreneur looking at his department, 'how, in the short term, can the existing transport system be organized to reduce the total cost of taking commuters from their homes to their workplaces?' and, for the longer term, 'in what way could the facilities be improved to remove bottlenecks?' or 'how might residential, commercial and industrial areas be arranged to reduce total travel effort?'. If he takes up these questions, the jargon will be different to to that of the entrepreneur, but the approach will be the same.

In this chapter attention will be focused on centralized planning. Thus, for the firm's specific problem of charging for transport, the analysis of production activities and the urban problem of satisfying community travel needs, the questions will be reduced to 'how can a central organizing body move goods which are supplied in given quantities at given points to other points where they are required in given quantities?'. A number of operational research techniques have been developed to cope with this question which has now become known as the *transportation problem*. Needless to say, they have a wide application to other problems. Some examples of these are route planning for a 'travelling salesman', where a unit has to choose an order in which to visit points in a transport system at the smallest possible travel cost, and manpower planning, where a workforce with a given range of skills and educational backgrounds has to be

Transport Planning

fitted into a given set of jobs. For the purpose here, though, the specific application will be to transportation itself.

6.1 The Transportation Problem

Both the transport department in the firm and the urban transport system can be considered as small productive organizations in their own right. Following the ideas of chapter 3, they will operate on the basis of minimizing cost for fixed output defined, now, in terms of goods delivered to given locations. Take, for example, three customers C_1, C_2 and C_3 who require 50, 100 and 200 units of finished goods respectively. Suppose that there are available, at two depots, D_1 and D_2, 250 and 200 units, and that the unit cost of transport between the depots and customers is given by adding costs along the links in Fig. 6.1. The problem would be to ask what arrangement of units from

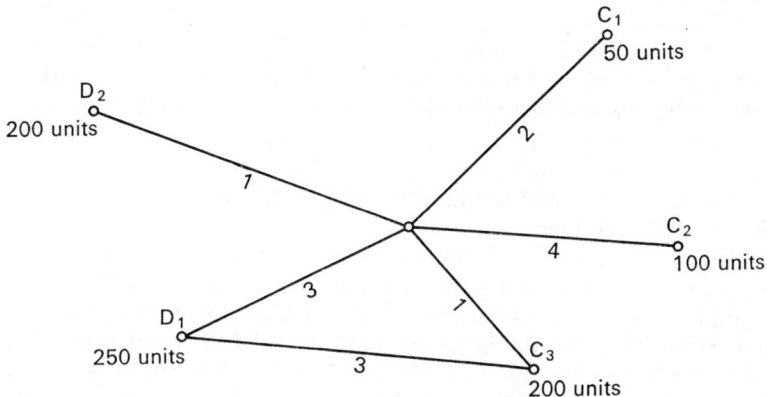

Fig. 6.1 Unit costs for transport between depots and customers.

depots to customers would both satisfy the customers and give the smallest total transport cost.

There are 6 ways in which goods can be delivered; either depot can supply each of the three customers. If the number of units transported from D_i to C_j is denoted by x_{ij}, $i = 1, 2, j = 1, 2, 3$ then the customer requirements could be given by the equations

$$x_{11} + x_{21} = 50$$
$$x_{12} + x_{22} = 100$$
$$x_{13} + x_{23} = 200$$

Also the available quantities at the depots provide restrictions on levels of the deliveries that share a common depot, and so

$$x_{11} + x_{12} + x_{13} \leqslant 250$$
$$x_{21} + x_{22} + x_{23} \leqslant 200$$

Finally, the total cost is given by

$$5x_{11} + 7x_{12} + 3x_{13} + 3x_{21} + 5x_{22} + 2x_{23}$$

This is the objective function for which the minimum value is to be sought over the non-negative variables x_{ij} whose values satisfy the above equality and inequality constraints.

The same formulation could be built up from transport problems in any of the stages of the firm's operation or, in fact, from the transport system as seen by the urban planner. The goods transported might just as easily be components, supplies, workers or shoppers. The only variation that could be considered involves the occurence of the equality and inequality signs in the five constraints. If the problem had been phrased, for example, in terms of disposing of supplies from depots with minimum requirements attached to the customers, then the equalities would be replaced by 'greater than or equal to' signs and inequalities by equalities. For the time being, though, as most of the development of the techniques has been derived from the operational problems of firms, the terminology will be left with finished goods, depots and customers.

The problem specified above resembles closely those that were earlier solved by the Simplex Method. In fact, the same technique could be used again. As the coefficients are all unity or zero and form the pattern that they do, however, a more straightforward method is available to find the optimal solution. For this, the variables x_{ij} are first arranged in the tableau of Table 6.1 where the rows and columns

TABLE 6.1
The tableau for the transportation problem

		C_1 50	C_2 100	C_3 200	C_4 100
D_1	250	5 x_{11}	7 x_{12}	3 x_{13}	0 x_{14}
D_2	200	3 x_{21}	5 x_{22}	2 x_{23}	0 x_{24}

line up with the supply and delivery totals. The surplus supply of 100 units is supposed written off to a fictitious customer C_4 at zero cost and is represented in the tableau by the new variables x_{14} and x_{24}. In the terminology of the previous chapters, these are two 'slack' variables which ensure that the row and column values add up exactly to the stipulations. The unit costs are also added to the tableau in the top left-hand corner of each cell.

Following the principles of the Simplex Method in the search for an optimum, the variables are to be grouped and regrouped under the classification of 'basic' and 'non-basic'. The Simplex tableau related the basic variables to the non-basic. Now the transportation problem imposes a number of constraints on the variables which serve a similar purpose. For example, in Table 6.1, once three values have been determined in any row, the fourth will follow. Also, at least one variable value must be chosen in each column so that the customer requirements can be met. In fact, the whole distribution can be determined by three variables and hence there are three degrees of freedom in the choice of all the values. (In general terms, with m rows and n columns, there will be $(m-1)(n-1)$ degrees of freedom.) Therefore there can be three 'independent' variables at any one time which, if they are set to zero, decide the values of the remaining five variables. (Generally there will be $m+n-1$ remaining.) Continuing with the Simplex principles, different sets of three variables will therefore have to be selected and set to zero. In each case the chosen variables will become 'non-basic' leaving the remainder 'basic', and the resulting patterns of variable values have to be tested for optimality. These patterns form 'basic feasible solutions' for the problem and at one of them at least an optimum will be found. The search for the optimum therefore requires the setting up of an initial solution and then concentrates on methodically moving from one solution to the next, each time reducing the value of total cost.

To construct an initial basic solution, the cells can be scanned in turn from left to right along each row, and values entered where appropriate. Starting at the top left-hand corner and moving along the top row, the largest possible value is placed in each cell. Zero values are not entered. Eventually in this way, a point will be reached where the top row supply total is met and the scan is then continued on the cell immediately below in the next row. The entries are again made using the largest possible positive values, and the scan moves to the right along this row until the supply constraint is satisfied. The procedure is repeated through all the rows until, at the end, all constraints are satisfied. For the example, this would mean the values 50, 100, 100, 100 and 100 being entered in the cells (1, 1), (1, 2), (1, 3), (2, 3) and (2, 4) to give the first tableau in Table 6.2. They are sufficient

TABLE 6.2

Successive tableaux in the solution of a transportation problem

1st tableau

		C_1 50	C_2 100	C_3 200	C_4 100	
D_1	250	5 50 b	7 100 b	3 100 b −100 n	0 1 +100	0
D_2	200	3 n	4 5 n	6 2 100 b +100	0 100 b −100	−1
		5	7	3	1	

2nd tableau

5 50 b	7 100 b −100	3 b +100	0 100 b	0
3 n	4 5 n +100	6 2 200 b −100	0 −1 n	−1
5	7	3	1	

3rd tableau

5 50 b −50 n	7 	6 3 100 b +50	0 100 b	0
3 n +50 b	4 5 100	2 100 b −50	0 −1 n	−1
5	6	3	0	

4th tableau

5 n	4 7 n	6 3 150 b	0 100 b	0
3 50 b	5 100 b	2 50 b	0 −1 n	−1
4	6	3	0	

Transport Planning 93

to make up the required totals and leave the variables x_{21}, x_{22} and x_{14} at value zero. These will be the current non-basic variables. The total allocation provides a basic solution which, as all the variables are non-negative, is also feasible.

This method of filling the cells is called the *north-west corner rule* and, when there are m rows and n columns, will always satisfy the row and column constraints with at most $m + n - 1$ positive values. If there were less than $m + n - 1$ positive values, the solution is called *degenerate* and some of the non-basic variables are chosen to make up the numbers. The way they would be selected can be seen from the next step.

Once a basic solution has been found, it must be checked for optimality. If it is not optimal, then the situation can be improved by moving towards another basic solution. Therefore, to check the first tableau, it will be necessary to see if any reorganization can make a cost saving, and in particular, if a move to another basic solution would cut costs. Such a move will mean exchanging a pair of variables, one from each of the basic and non-basic categories. The choice is illustrated in the first tableau of Table 6.2 by labelling the variables in each category '*b*' and '*n*' as appropriate. The consequences of different exchanges can be indicated by setting up a set of values, one for each row and one for each column, called *shadow costs*. They are added to Table 6.2 in such a way that the actual cost value in a basic cell is equal to the sum of the shadow cost values for the row and column in which that cell is placed. By convention, the first row is assigned the value zero and then, in the example, column values are put equal to the costs in their first row cells if there is a basic variable there. Columns 1, 2 and 3 therefore have values 5, 7 and 3. Next, the shadow cost for the second row is constructed to add up to the cost 2 in the cell for variable x_{23}. It will equal -1. Finally, the shadow cost for the fourth column will be 1 to add the second row value of -1 and give the zero total for the cell of variable x_{24}. If there had been less than $m + n - 1$ basic variables, this evaluation of shadow costs could not have been completed. Therefore, when some non-basic variables are changed to basic to make up the required number, they will be chosen so that the shadow costs can all be found.

The shadow costs indicate the result of unit increases in the non-basic variables and hence provide both a test for an optimal solution and an indication of how a non-optimal solution can be improved. For each non-basic variable cell in Table 6.2 the sum of the shadow costs for the row and column is placed in the top right-hand corner. If this value is greater than the actual cost for the cell, then the total cost of the distribution of deliveries will be reduced if that cell value is increased. Of course, to balance the totals, other cell values will have to be adjusted and, if these changes are confined to basic variables, the difference between the sum of the shadow costs and the actual cost provides the resulting unit change in cost. In the example, the cell for variable x_{14} has a shadow cost sum of 1, compared with a zero actual cost. If some units are moved to that cell by adjustments in the basic variables x_{13}, x_{23} and x_{24}, the unit saving in cost will be $1 - 0 = 1$. If the sum had been less than or equal to the actual cost, then no improvement could be immediately gained from such a reorganization.

Table 6.2 shows how a series of changes have been made from the initial basic solution to the optimum. At each stage the variables are

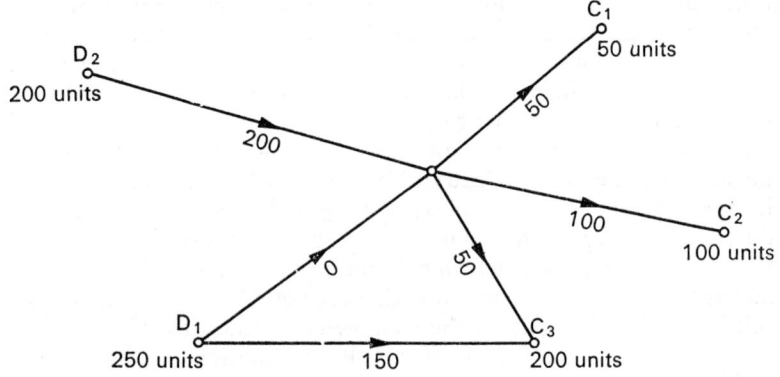

Fig. 6.2 The optimal distribution between depots and customers.

split into basic and non-basic categories and the shadow costs constructed. If there is an improvement possible by adding to a non-basic variable cell, then as many units are moved there as can be taken from the basic variables. This will ensure that as large an improvement as possible is made at each step, and that, while the non-basic variable becomes basic, one of the basic variables takes its place. Finally, when the fourth tableau is reached, the shadow cost sums are all at least as large as the actual costs. The solution cannot be improved and therefore represents the optimal distribution pattern. If this is related back to the original problem specification in Fig. 6.1, then the numbers of units despatched through the transport system will be those attached to the links in Fig. 6.2.

The only time when there is likely to be any difficulty in making the moves from one tableau to the next is where some non-basic variables have their status changed to basic so that the quota of basic variables can be maintained. It is then possible that the circuit of alterations

Transport Planning

requires something taken away from a zero basic variable cell. In this case, the shadow costs would be recalculated using the non-basic variable for whose benefit the circuit was constructed, as a basic variable. This then replaces the other zero basic variable which is put back into the non-basic category.

6.2 The Interpretation of Shadow Costs

The shadow costs are introduced in the transportation problem to provide a mechanism for testing a basic solution for optimality. It can be shown that they have the same interpretation as the imputed values discussed in the context of the Simplex Method. They provide a marginal valuation on possible changes in the non-basic variables.

Consider the ith and kth rows and the jth and lth columns of a transportation problem tableau. Suppose that the variable x_{ij} is currently non-basic, the variables x_{kj}, x_{kl} and x_{il} are basic and the shadow costs associated with the rows and columns are u_i, u_k, v_j and v_l (see Table 6.3). Then, if c_{ij}, c_{il}, c_{kj} and c_{kl} are the actual costs associated with the cells, by construction

$$u_i + v_l = c_{il}$$
$$u_k + v_l = c_{kl}$$
$$u_k + v_j = c_{kj}$$

TABLE 6.3

Derivation and use of shadow costs

	C_j	C_l	
D_i	c_{ij} n	c_{il} x_{il} b	v_i
D_k	c_{kj} x_{kj} b	c_{kl} x_{kl} b	v_k
	u_j	u_l	

The basic cells for which these equalities apply provide a circuit round the non-basic variable x_{ij}. When there are $m + n - 1$ basic variables in the tableau, some circuit like this can always be drawn through the basic variables. It may not, though, be as simple as this one, and may include more than three 'stepping stones'.

The rule for checking optimality is that an improvement can be made by increasing the value of variable x_{ij} if

$$u_i + v_j > c_{ij}$$

Substituting from the above equations

$$c_{ij} - c_{il} + c_{kl} - c_{kj} < 0$$

which shows that the change in total cost arising from the redistribution of a unit around the cells is less than zero.

The implication of the rule is that, if for all cells (i, j)

$$u_i + v_j \leqslant c_{ij}$$

then no improvement could be found by any redistribution. It will obviously follow if a circuit contained only basic variables, but suppose that a redistribution is possible around one with some non-basic variables in it. An incremental change around the circuit would mean taking a value away from the basic variable cells, and adding to both non-basic and basic variable cells. The combined unit effect on total cost will then be

$$c_{ij} - c_{il} + c_{kl} - c_{kj} \geqslant (u_i + v_j) - c_{il} + (u_k + v_l) - c_{kj}$$

which, by definition of the shadow costs,

$$\geqslant (u_i + v_j) - (u_i + v_l) + (u_k + v_l) - (u_k + v_j)$$
$$= 0$$

and so the redistribution will not lead to a decrease in cost. The shadow costs therefore provide a quick method of testing for improvements by any possible redistribution.

Besides indicating the marginal changes in cost that arise from redistributions within the current row and column totals, the shadow costs can be used to indicate the effect of changing the totals themselves. Suppose that, when an optimal distribution has been reached, the totals for the row i and column j are increased by a small amount δ. To remedy the immediate imbalance in the table, the same amount can be added to the cell (i, j). The shadow costs will not be affected and, if the variable x_{ij} is basic, then the solution will be optimal, and the extra cost incurred is $c_{ij}\delta = (u_i^0 + v_j^0)\delta$. Otherwise, if it is non-basic, then a situation would have been reached that is a small move away from an optimal distribution. The optimum can be restored by redistributing the extra amount δ round a circuit of basic variables. Doing this will decrease the cost by an amount $(c_{ij} - u_i^0 - v_j^0)\delta$ and therefore the total increase in cost from the beginning will be $(u_i^0 + v_j^0)\delta$. This is simply the sum of one contribution from the origin i and one from the destination j. Hence the extra cost of delivering one more unit to customer C_j and simultaneously taking one from the supply at depot D_i is the sum, $(u_i^0 + v_j^0)$, of shadow costs attached to the customer and depot.

Suppose now that a firm is looking at its policy of charging for transport, and that the cost of a unit of the goods is p_i at depot D_i while the price to the customer C_j is p_j. The transport charge will be $(p_j - p_i)$. If the customer wants an extra unit from that depot, the extra cost of transport will be $(u_i^0 + v_j^0)$. Therefore, if $p_j - p_i > u_i^0 + v_j^0$, then the carriage of such goods is to be encouraged in the future, and, if $p_j - p_i < u_i^0 + v_j^0$, it is to be discouraged. The cost, $(u_i^0 + v_j^0)$, gives a more accurate representation of carriage costs than the constant c_{ij} itself because it allows for a reassignment of all deliveries to accommodate the extra unit. This is particularly useful as well when prices have not been determined. Then it is possible to use the system to set the charges $(p_j - p_i)$ according to the shadow costs, thus ensuring a profitable set of operations.

In the long term, under perfect competition, it could be expected that the profit-maximizing firm would alter its prices to a point of zero profit for all deliveries. In that case, the geographical price pattern would end up looking like the shadow costs themselves, viz.

$$p_i = c - u_i^0$$
$$p_j = c + v_j^0$$

where c is a constant determined by the actual production process. At these prices all deliveries will be made at zero profit, the total revenue obtained in the price mark-ups between depots and customers being entirely absorbed in total cost. Further, it will be an equilibrium profit, for no unused method of delivery has a cost in excess of the price mark-up. It will be seen in chapter 8 that such long-term price patterns are particularly relevant in urban planning with emphasis being placed on the locational advantage of different areas with regard to access to markets, commuting and shopping. For the present, though, the discussion will continue by concentrating on the use of the actual transport network.

6.3 Problems of Traffic Planning

The example above involved one firm organizing its own transportation within a fixed transport network. Now consider operation of the transport system itself as it copes with several such transport departments, either from the point of view of a centralized organization serving companies within a group, or a separate public or private carrier meeting the transport needs of its customers. The problem then will be to satisfy a set of fixed demands for transport at the smallest cost to the carrier.

Consider an example, described in Fig. 6.3, of a 5-link network joining 4 towns, A_1, A_2, A_3 and A_4 between which two firms wish to

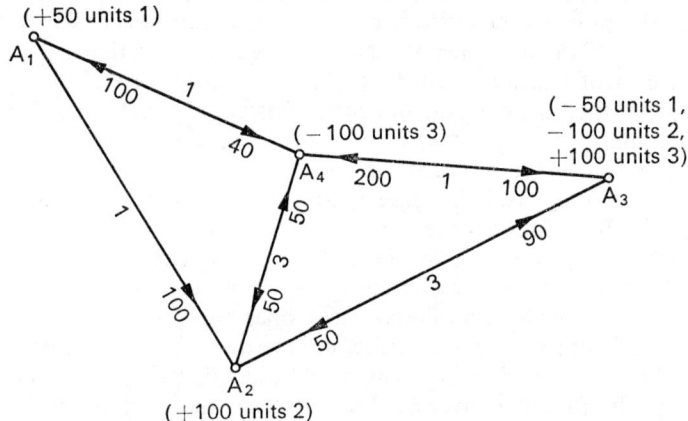

Fig. 6.3 Link capacities and unit costs for transportation through a transport system.

transport their goods. A day's schedule consists of firm 1 wishing to move 50 units from its depot at A_1 to a customer at A_3, and firm 2 wishing to move 100 units from A_2 to A_3 and 100 units from A_3 to A_4. (Each consignment is referred to as a different good, numbered 1, 2 and 3 respectively, and is recorded in the figure by requirements (−) and available quantities (+) in round brackets next to the appropriate nodes.) Suppose the carrier operates vehicles daily in the direction of the arrows, and provides the given load capacities. Suppose also that he reckons his unit costs along the links to be 1, 1, 3, 3 and 1. The particular problem that faces him is arranging his vehicle loads so that he satisfies the customers at the smallest cost to himself.

The same techniques as those used earlier will help find the optimal daily loadings. The application is, though, more complicated and relies on four interlinked tableaux shown in Table 6.4. For Firm 1 an array of loads x_{ij1} indicates how much of good 1 is transported along the links between towns A_i and A_j. The diagonal cells are given a

TABLE 6.4
Four interlinked tableaux showing an optimal solution to the allocation of daily loadings

Firm 1—good 1

		A_1 $N(+0 \cdot 01)$		A_2 $N(+0 \cdot 01)$		A_3 $50 + N(+0 \cdot 01)$		A_4 $N(+0 \cdot 41)$	
			0		1		m		1	
A_1	$50 + N(+0 \cdot 1)$	$N(+0 \cdot 01)$		$10(-0 \cdot 31)$			3	$40(+0 \cdot 4)$	5	0
A_2	$N(+0 \cdot 1)$		-1 0	$N - 10(+0 \cdot 32)$				$10(-0 \cdot 22)$	3 3	-1
A_3	$N(+0 \cdot 1)$		-5 3			$N(+0 \cdot 1)$	-4 0		-1 1	-2
A_4	$N(+0 \cdot 14)$		-4 3			$50(-0 \cdot 09)$	-3 1	$N - 50(+0 \cdot 23)$	0	-1
		0		1		2		1		

Firm 2—good 2

		$N(+0 \cdot 01)$		$N(+0 \cdot 01)$		$100 + N(+0 \cdot 01)$		$N(+0 \cdot 41)$	
			0		1		m		1	
A_1	$N(+0 \cdot 1)$	$N(+0 \cdot 01)$		$(+0 \cdot 09)$			3		5 1	0
A_2	$100 + N(+0 \cdot 1)$		-1 0	$N(-0 \cdot 08)$		90		$10(+0 \cdot 18)$	3	-1
A_3	$N(+0 \cdot 1)$		-5 3			$N(+0 \cdot 1)$	-4 0		-1 1	-2
A_4	$N(+0 \cdot 14)$		-4 3			$10(-0 \cdot 09)$	-3 1	$N - 10(+0 \cdot 23)$	0	-1
		0		1		2		1		

Firm 2—good 3

		$N(+0 \cdot 01)$		$N(+0 \cdot 01)$		$N(+0 \cdot 01)$		$100 + N(+0 \cdot 41)$	
			0		1		m		1	
A_1	$N(+0 \cdot 1)$	$N(+0 \cdot 01)$		$(+0 \cdot 09)$			3		3 1	0
A_2	$N(+0 \cdot 1)$		-1 0	$N(-0 \cdot 08)$				$(+0 \cdot 18)$	1 3	-1
A_3	$100 + N(+0 \cdot 1)$		-3 3			$N(+0 \cdot 1)$	-2 0	$100(+0 \cdot 09)$	1	0
A_4	$N(+0 \cdot 14)$		-4 3				-3 1	$N(+0 \cdot 14)$	-1 0	-1
		0		1		0		1		

TABLE 6.4 (continued)

Surplus capacity

	$N + 2P + 100(+0.01)$		$N + 200(+0.01)$		$N + P + 40(+0.01)$		$N + 190(+0.41)$	
A_1 $N + P + 90(+0.1)$	0	0	90(+0.4)	0	P	0	−3	0
A_2 $N + P + 40(+0.1)$	$N(−0.03)$	0	$N + 10(−0.10)$	0		−1	30(+0.26)	0
A_3 $N + P + 150(+0.1)$	P	0	50	0	$N(−0.21)$	0	100(+0.31)	3
A_4 $N + 250(+0.14)$	P	0	50(+0.04)	0	40(+0.22)	0	$N + 60(−0.16)$	3
	100(+0.04)							
	0		0		−3		−3	

Total capacity

A_1	$4N$	100	P	40(+0.4)
A_2	P	$4N$	90	50(+0.4)
A_3	P	50	$4N$	200(+0.4)
A_4	100(+0.04)	50(+0.04)	100(+0.04)	$4N(+0.44)$

Shadow costs across tableaux

	0	0	3	0
	0	0	2	3
	−3	−3	0	0
	−3	−3	0	0

Transport Planning

large value N which provides a reservoir of loads to avoid negative values in the tableau. So that these values do not interfere with total cost, the cells are given a zero cost. They will, though, have to be included in the row and column totals, which show, above and beyond the value N, where the goods have to be collected and delivered. Finally, the costs associated with the links are noted in the top left-hand corner of the off-diagonal cells, and, where no link directly joins two towns, a large cost value m is assumed.

Besides the tableau for firm 1–good 1, there are two other tableaux associated with goods 2 and 3 each having the same interpretation. The variables involved, x_{ij2} and x_{ij3}, are constrained, though, by different row and column totals each explaining the origin and destination of the goods. Altogether, the first three tableaux can be summarized by the equations

$$\sum_{j=1}^{4} x_{ijk} = a_{ik} + N, \, k = 1, 2, 3$$

and

$$\sum_{i=1}^{4} x_{ijk} = b_{jk} + N, \, k = 1, 2, 3$$

where a_{ik} are the given origin totals and b_{jk} the destination totals for good k.

The fourth tableau, an array of variables x_{ij4}, takes up the slack capacity along the links, and absorbs the spare vehicle loads with imaginary goods at zero cost. An arbitrary capacity P is assumed where no link exists. If the link capacities are d_{ij}, then the variables will also be constrained by the equations

$$\sum_{k=1}^{4} x_{ijk} = d_{ij}, \, i, j = 1, 2, 3, 4$$

where, in particular $d_{ii} = 4N$, $i = 1, 2, 3, 4$.
This implies that the variables in the fourth tableau are constrained by their own row and column totals

$$\sum_{j=1}^{4} x_{ij4} = N + \sum_{j=1}^{4} d_{ij} - \sum_{k=1}^{3} a_{ik}, \, i = 1, 2, 3, 4$$

and

$$\sum_{i=1}^{4} x_{ij4} = N + \sum_{i=1}^{4} d_{ij} - \sum_{k=1}^{3} b_{jk}, \, j = 1, 2, 3, 4$$

The problem centres on finding non-negative values for the variables x_{ijk} that satisfy all the constraints and provide the smallest total cost,

$$\sum_{i=1}^{4} \sum_{j=1}^{4} \sum_{k=1}^{3} c_{ijk} x_{ijk}$$

Some extra values have been added to the tableau in round brackets. One of the problems with setting up basic solutions for the four tableaux is the possibility of a small number of basic variables satisfying the constraints. If there are m rows, n columns and p tableaux there will be mnp variables overall. Of these, $(m-1)(n-1)(p-1)$ would be expected to be non-basic, the others basic. If there are less positive values in a particular solution than the required number of basic variables, then the solution is degenerate and it will not be possible to construct a full set of shadow costs. When this happened before, it was easy to convert some of the variables in the zero-valued cells to this basic category. Now it is difficult and a different, more systematic, method is required. This involves adding small values to the row, column and tableaux totals to ensure that no sub-total equals a sub-total from either of the other two sets of totals. To do this, multiples of 0·1 and 0·01 are added, and the cell values suitably increased. Then there will be exactly the right number of positive values.

If the first basic solution for the four tableaux is constructed by using the north-west corner rule across each tableau as well as through the tableaux, a set of shadow costs can be constructed to search for an improvement. Those associated with the rows are denoted by the variables u_{ik}, those with the columns by v_{jk} and those with the tableaux w_{ij}, and they will be arranged so that, for the basic variables,

$$u_{ik} + v_{jk} + w_{ij} = c_{ijk}$$

There will be $(mnp - (m-1)(n-1)(p-1)) = (mn + np + mp - m - n - p + 1)$ such equations in the $(mn + np + mp)$ shadow costs, and hence $(m + n + p - 1)$ costs will be undetermined. Initially these costs are zeroed and the remaining values deduced from them in the tableaux.

As before, if for some non-basic cell

$$u_{ik} + v_{jk} + w_{ij} > c_{ijk}$$

then an improvement in total cost can be gained by increasing the value of that variable. To make the adjustment, circuits will have to be constructed through the basic variables, and as many loads reorganized as possible. This will ensure that, while one variable leaves

Transport Planning 103

the non-basic group, another joins. Alternatively, if for all non-basic cells,

$$u_{ik} + v_{jk} + w_{ij} \leqslant c_{ijk}$$

then the solution will be optimal. Such a solution is shown in Table 6.4.

In the long term, the shadow costs indicate where the transport facilities might be changed or business expanded. In particular, the costs u_{ik}, v_{jk} and w_{ij} provide the change in total cost that result from unit changes in the constraint constants, i.e. the origin totals, the destination totals and the capacities. Therefore the sum for one of the cells in the first three tableaux, i.e. $(u_{ik} + v_{jk} + w_{ij})$ where $k = 1, 2, 3$ indicates the increase in total cost from simultaneous unit increases in the loads leaving A_i and arriving at A_j, and in the capacity of link (i, j). Also, as the goods in the fourth tableau are imaginary, added to take up the slack loads, the sum for the cells in that tableau, i.e. $(u_{i4} + v_{j4} + w_{ij})$ indicates simply the effect of a unit increase in the capacity of link (i, j). By subtracting these two sums, it is then possible to evaluate the effect of taking on more business between the two towns A_i and A_j. This is the marginal cost of transport to the carrier between A_i and A_j. He would be expected to adjust his business between those towns until the price he charged for his services equals the marginal cost.

In the example, the optimal set of tableaux would indicate that marginal loads of good 1, say, between towns A_1 and A_3 could be carried at a cost of $5 - 0 = 5$ (i.e., the difference between the shadow cost sums for cells (1, 3) in tableaux 1 and 4). For pricing purposes this will be his current marginal cost figure. It is a fortunate one for him and Fig. 6.4 shows why. There, the optimal solution is superimposed on the diagram of link costs, node requirements and available quantities. Marginal loads between the two towns will have to be carried via towns A_2 and A_4 at a cost of 5 whereas some loads are carried along links (1, 4) and (4, 3) at a cost to the carrier of 2. Therefore, as a result of link capacities, charging at the current marginal rate can create a positive profit.

A final question about the distribution concerns firm 2's attitude towards distinguishing between what it has called goods 2 and 3. If it were to allow substitution between the two goods, then it would be important to determine whether a different allocation might reduce transport costs. In the example, if some demands and supplies of good 2 in the second tableau were transferred to good 3 in the third tableau without a change in the capacities, it would be possible, by reorganizing the loads, to make a cost saving. This would be equal to the difference in shadow cost for the elements $(i, j, k) = (2, 3, 2)$ and

(2, 3, 3), i.e. $3 - 1 = 2$. It can be checked by examining Fig. 5.4 and noting that demand at A_4 would be satisfied by the supply from A_2, and the demand at A_3 by its own supply. Therefore, there will be an overall saving if firm 2 substituted between its goods.

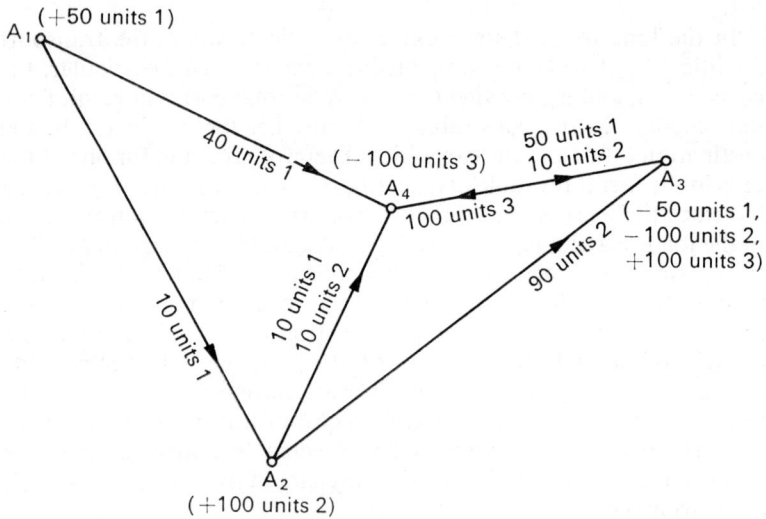

Fig. 6.4 Illustration of the optimal solution for the distribution of loads through the transport system.

6.4 Application to Urban Planning Problems

So far, discussions have been centred on the optimal distribution of transport loadings in industrial applications although they equally apply to public activities such as commuting to work. In this particular case, the problem would be the organization of the total 'rush-hour' commuting seen as a set of requirements on moves, from each home to each workplace, through a capacitated network of transport routes. The immediate question would concern the individual routings that minimize total travel cost. This is a desirable short-term solution from a community point of view with everyone's costs being considered just as important as anyone else's. On the other hand, though, the long-term question asks whether 'substitution' between homes and workplaces would produce more economical pairings of origins and destinations. This then goes back to the first transportation problem where there was one homogeneous good, all the commuters being interchangeable. Therefore the two formulations in this chapter can

Transport Planning

help the urban planner search for what is best over the time horizons in which he is interested. What they do not do, though, is describe how commuters behave.

It is generally considered that patterns of distribution found in actual situations follow a 'law of gravitation'. The interchange t_{ij} between origins i and destinations j can be fitted to a model

$$t_{ij} = a_i b_j f(d_{ij})$$

where a_i and b_j are factors associated with particular origins and destinations, and $f(d_{ij})$ is a function representing the effect of their separation. Traditionally, the constants a_i and b_j have been interpreted as the power of specific locations to generate and attract commuters, trips or trade, and the equation represents an equilibrium where demand for and supply of travel are matched. Alternatively, if the model is used to describe the distribution of a fixed travel demand, the a_i and b_j values become balancing factors that ensure the origin and destination targets are met. In either form, the explanations of the model are varied and its applicability seems very wide. Its importance here lies in its power to distribute values in the transportation tableau. The point is that the pattern is not necessarily the optimum indicated by the transportation problem. So, the planner is set a real problem to sort out with the reorganization of traffic flows, and he would seem to be assured that there is a positive reward to be gained from it.

7 Traffic Control

A major problem for an organizing body is the implementation of its plans. In the previous chapter the assumption was made that some central body had complete control over the system and could make whatever changes it liked. It is, however, more realistic to recognize that usually decision-making is decentralized. In a number of areas, particularly those involving traffic movement, the people who take the decisions, e.g. commuters, have their own behaviour patterns centring round individual objectives. If they are to be persuaded to fit into an overall plan, the central body will have to consider what conditions must be created to make their objectives coincide with its own. The success of the implementation will depend on the extent to which this can be done.

At the end of the last chapter it was mentioned that commuters do not appear to choose distribution patterns that are optimal in the sense of centralized transport planning. The main reasons for their behaviour are deep-rooted in locational preferences and are difficult to disentangle. A simplified case study can be found, however, by concentrating on the assignment of individual loads, or commuters, to routes in a transport network. Although not all the features of the distribution will be present, there is still sufficient material for discussion. Quite simply, demand for journeys with particular origins and destinations is supposed to be given by a function of travel time, and the questions revolve around the routings chosen through the road network for a relatively large number of loads. Generally, if no controls are imposed, congestion will occur on the preferred routes. This can be shown to be inefficient from an overall community point of view requiring more travel effort in total than it need do if some central organization were imposed. The planner's problem is to decide how to control the traffic to encourage an assignment of routes that is nearer the optimum.

The control amounts to rationing out the road capacity. In the following sections, four methods are considered involving bid and ballot systems, congestion of road space itself, and the choice of time of travel. They each illustrate different aspects of decentralized decision-making and, although they look at a narrow traffic problem,

Traffic Control

they can be applied more generally to industrial or urban situations where congestion can occur.

7.1 A Bid System

One method of allocating routes would be simply to hold an auction. To illustrate this, suppose there are two routes, A and B, of equal flow capacity c both connecting the same two towns. In addition route A is shorter in length than route B and hence is less time-consuming. Therefore, as the traffic flow between the two towns builds up, the flow along route A will reach capacity and the only choice for the remaining loads is to use route B. At a later stage, route B will be at capacity and the remaining loads prevented from travelling through the road network at all. To avoid confusion over who follows which route within a given time period, suppose that tickets are auctioned in front of all the operators. The result that would be expected is that the fixed number of tickets for routes A and B would be sold at prices which their buyers consider worthwhile, equal to or below the value to them as individual operators. Further, anyone who could not 'afford' to buy a ticket for route A, say, at the prices asked would have judged the prices to be equal to or exceed the value he put on the use of route A. So all the operators will be satisfied with the allocation. Moreover, there will be no congestion on the routes, which work to capacity when there is sufficient demand, and, since there is then no wasted travel effort, the allocation could be said to be 'efficient'.

In effect, the price system is a rationing device where some of the advantage of a particular route is drawn away from the operators for some communal use. Depending on how the bidding is actually conducted, the operators will each find the value of a ticket that is bought equals or exceeds its price. If there is a difference, it represents the surplus benefit that he obtains from carrying the load. In other words, it is his personal trading profit realized not necessarily in cash terms, but in terms of worth to himself. The sum of all surpluses is known as *consumer surplus*. The method of bidding that provides the largest value of consumer surplus for this situation is that of a central body announcing prices from day to day and waiting for the operators to put in their requirements. This way, a market price for each route could be derived. The relationship between such prices and the total number, n, of potential operators is given in Fig. 7.1. As the number increases there is more likelihood of there being more operators who value carrying the load highly. Therefore a higher price would be expected.

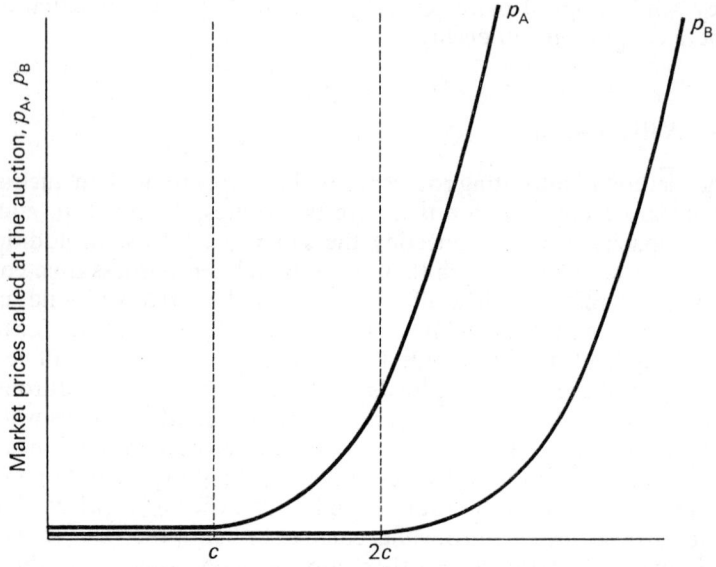

Fig. 7.1 Relationship between market prices and total number of operators for a bid system.

7.2 A Ballot System

Since congestion inevitably occurs when a large number of similar people wish to use a facility, it is quite likely that the above bid system will not be valid. If, say, everyone put forward the same bid, then the mechanism will still not sort out exactly c loads for each of the routes. Instead of relying on a price system, lots could be drawn on the basis of one chance per load. The alternatives and probabilities would then be those given in Table 7.1 where M is a heavy time penalty associated with the next alternative. The resulting movement of loads would be efficient from the point of view of total time-cost, and the individual operators would each be faced with the same expectation at the outset. This is illustrated in Fig. 7.2 for different numbers of loads.

The expected time-cost, $\bar{t}$, provides a measure by which the operators can judge the effort of transporting loads. It is therefore a good basis for a demand curve. If a count is made of the number of loads that it is worthwhile trying to transport for a given expected cost, a demand relationship can be derived between $\bar{t}$ and n. This is imposed on Fig. 7.2, and the point of intersection with the expected time-cost as

Traffic Control

TABLE 7.1
Probabilities of alternative outcomes for an operator under a ballot system

		Outcome of ballot		
		route A	route B	not travel
time-cost		t_A	t_B	M
Probability	if $n \leqslant c$	1	0	0
	if $c \leqslant n \leqslant 2c$	$\dfrac{c}{n}$	$\dfrac{n-c}{n}$	0
	if $n \geqslant 2c$	$\dfrac{c}{n}$	$\dfrac{c}{n}$	$\dfrac{n-2c}{n}$

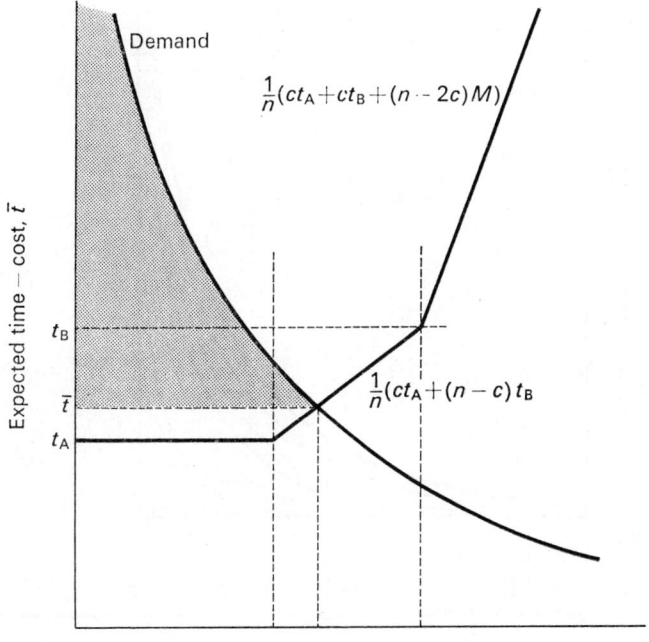

n, total number of operators

Fig. 7.2 An operators view of expected cost in a ballot system.

supplied by the routes is the solution towards which the situation will gravitate. Moreover, the size of the shaded area beneath the demand curve and above the cost line is equal to the consumer surplus at the equilibrium solution and provides a means by which it can be visualized.

7.3 Congestion of Road Space

One of the most effective methods of rationing is provided unaided by the traffic congestion itself. A well-used representation of traffic flow along road links is a queuing model. The links can be thought of as a series of restrictions at each of which small queues form. The arrival of vehicles at the beginning of the links is likely to be erratic, somewhere between the extremes of purely random and equi-spaced arrivals and the resulting time–costs that operators can expect for the road links are shown in Fig. 7.3. The curves are constructed by imagining that the road link has been operating at the same flow level

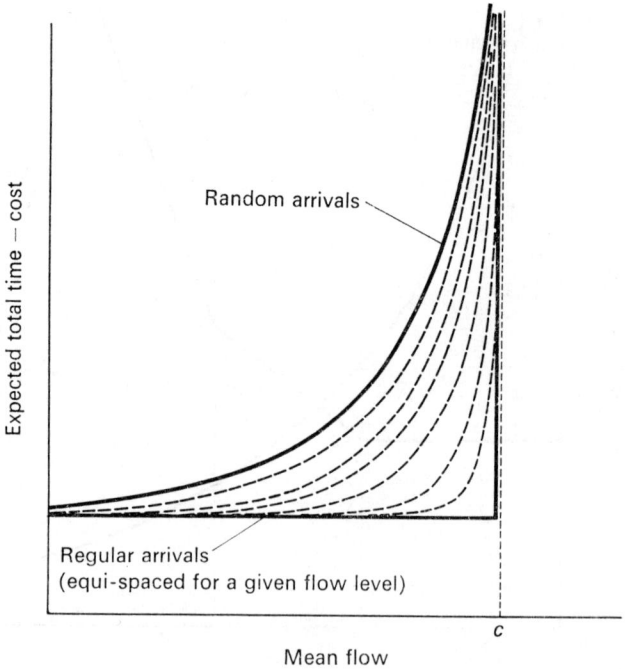

Fig. 7.3 A queuing model of traffic congestion; expected time-cost against mean flow.

for a long time and they show the delay that a particular vehicle can expect to experience when it arrives. This is only an average figure and the actual delay will be determined largely by the arrival pattern immediately prior to the vehicle's arrival. When a driver starts a journey, however, it is as though he takes a delay out of a hat, the average delay of all those in the hat being the expected value on the curve. The curves will be upward sloping with increasing flow rates, and lie between those two named in the figure.

Therefore it will be possible to place some definable time–flow relationships on all links in a transport network and so provide a basis for an allocation of loads to the different routes between origins and destinations. It would be expected that, at this allocation, the expected delays due to congestion on a particular route would be sufficient to deter all those loads that are not sent, and would not be sufficient to deter all those that are sent. Therefore, just as the bid and ballot system set criteria by which alternative routes can be assessed, so congestion itself provides a possible system of costing with a 'market price' measured in terms of travel time, rather than money, and placed on each link which could be used. The questions that are left to examine ask whether such an allocation actually exists whatever the complexity of the transport network, whether it is efficient in terms of total transport cost, and, if it is not, what modifications can be made to the system.

Before considering a general transport network, the simple example of two routes between two towns provides a useful discussion point. Suppose that all loads end up at the same destination and split between the routes A and B according to the flows x_A and x_B. Total flow is $x = x_A + x_B$. If congestion is allowed on the links, the level of flows will dictate the travel times for the routes. If the expected times are denoted by y_A and y_B, then, where h_A and h_B are time–flow relationships of the type discussed above,

$$y_A = h_A(x_A)$$

and

$$y_B = h_B(x_B)$$

As is shown in the first diagram of Fig. 7.4, when the flows are zero the expected times will equal the times t_A and t_B respectively, and when they approach the capacity c the times become very large.

In their turn the expected journey times along the routes will influence demand for travel. The number of journeys made could be derived by considering total travel effort as a balanced collection of two factors in the expression

$$y + p(y)/b$$

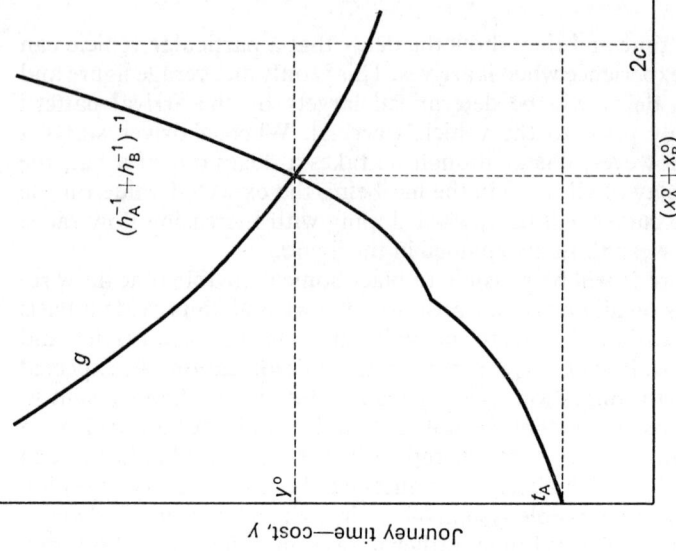
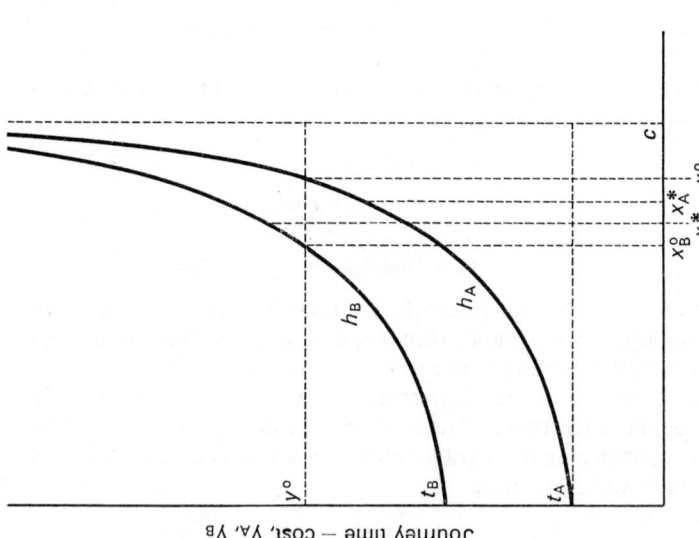

Fig. 7.4 The solution for the division of traffic between routes A and B by congestion.

where y is the expected journey time, p is a function which gives the money cost of carrying a unit load for that time, and b is the traveller's current money cost/journey time trade-off at the present point on his indifference curves. This will depend on his overall situation beyond immediate decisions on transport, and would be expected to vary from person to person. The assumption is often made, though, that it is constant over the travelling population, at least over those using the road system. (It is not unusual to see a 'generalized' cost inserted here incorporating other trade-offs which involve, for example, comfort or reliability. These could be justified by stipulating 'standards' which the traveller expects of the service and then applying the generalized arguments of chapter 2 to extract marginal valuations that can be placed on those features. These will provide the necessary trade-offs. A major objection to this is that it introduces too many individual assessments into travel effort which will therefore take on a quite different value over travellers that make up the flow.) Altogether, the value of the expression for travel effort will indicate the amount by which demand is suppressed. The total number of loads transported would be a decreasing function of effort and, if an inverse function is constructed (A15), it will be possible to trace back through demand to find the effort level that will cut off a given number of loads. Going one stage further and interpreting travel effort in terms of expected journey time y, the function g can be defined to give the travel time between the towns which cuts off a flow of x loads,

$$y = g(x)$$

The time–flow and demand relationships provide a means of expressing the conditions that define an equilibrium allocation to the routes. If there is flow along both routes, then the travel times would be expected to be equal and if there is flow along just one route, the travel time along the other would be expected to be greater. Otherwise, the expected cause of no flow along a route would be a travel time that is too great. An acceptable level of travel time is one which together with the flow rates satisfies both the time–flow and demand relationships, and the full conditions can be summarized as follows,

$$x_A > 0 \quad \text{implies} \quad y = g(x) = h_A(x_A)$$
$$x_B > 0 \quad \text{implies} \quad y = g(x) = h_B(x_B)$$
$$h_A(x_A) > g(x) \text{ implies } x_A = 0$$

and

$$h_B(x_B) > g(x) \text{ implies } x_B = 0$$

where $x = x_A + x_B$.

The equilibrium solution is illustrated in Fig. 7.4 and can be derived by examining the two parts. Fig. 7.4(a) contains the two time–flow relationships, and if both routes are used, and hence the travel times are equal at y, say, then the flow levels will be x_A^0 and x_B^0 respectively. In diagram b a new curve is drawn relating the sum of the flows $(x_A^0 + x_B^0)$ that would be expected through the network if the travel time on both routes were equal to y. It is denoted in the convention of inverse functions (A15) as $(h_A^{-1} + h_B^{-1})^{-1}$. The point where this curve cuts total demand between the origin and destination corresponds to the equilibrium solution. At any level to the left of this point, the routes will be less crowded than the travellers expect and, to the right, more crowded. They would therefore be expected to adjust their loadings towards the equilibrium.

The equilibrium conditions, phrased as they are above, resemble a set of conditions associated with an optimal solution. If a special function H is constructed using the integrals (A16) of the time–flow and demand relationships, i.e.

$$H \equiv \int_0^{x_A + x_B} g(x)\, dx - \int_0^{x_A} h_A(x)\, dx - \int_0^{x_B} h_B(x)\, dx$$

then the partial derivatives with respect to the flow levels will be

$$\frac{\delta H}{\delta x_A} = g(x_A + x_B) - h_A(x_A)$$

and

$$\frac{\delta H}{\delta x_B} = g(x_A + x_B) - h_B(x_B)$$

Therefore, as long as the function H obeys the necessary assumptions of concavity, the Kuhn–Tucker conditions can be used to examine the properties of the maximum point that is contained within the restriction of non-negative flows, i.e. within the region $x_A, x_B \geqslant 0$. They will specify that

$$x_A^0 > 0 \text{ implies } \frac{\delta H}{\delta x_A} = 0$$

and

$$\frac{\delta H}{\delta x_A} < 0 \text{ implies } x_A^0 = 0$$

for route A, and a similar pair of conditions for route B at the optimal point, (x_A^0, x_B^0). These are precisely the equilibrium conditions stated above and so the equilibrium solution coincides with the maximum solution for the function H.

By itself the coincidence of the two solutions is not very interesting.

Traffic Control

It does, though, give a clue to the question of existence of an equilibrium solution in the general case. Consider a road network consisting of links ij that connect together to form routes between origins and destinations. They are usually two-way, carrying loads which are intended for destinations k, $k = 1, 2, 3, \ldots$, and the flow level in the direction i to j is non-negative and denoted by $x_{ij,k} \geqslant 0$. Define total flow along link ij by

$$x_{ij} = \sum_k x_{ij,k} \geq 0$$

and the flow originating at node i destined for node k as

$$x_{i,k} \equiv \sum_j (x_{ij,k} - x_{ji,k})$$

Also, suppose the time–flow relationship for each link relates the expected journey time for that link, y_{ij}, to the flow level,

$$y_{ij} = h_{ij}(x_{ij})$$

where h_{ij} is a suitable function derived from a queueing model. Time can then be assued to be increasing with the number of loads carried along the link and reaches greater and greater values as the flow approaches capacity of the link, c_{ij}, say. Finally, suppose that the inverted demand relationship for travel between two nodes i and k is given by

$$y_{i,k} = g_{i,k}(x_{i,k})$$

where $y_{i,k}$ is the expected journey time along the shortest path between the nodes and $g_{i,k}$ is a decreasing function that is never less than zero. It is assumed that the journey time along all competing paths are known to the travellers who are able to choose those with the smallest expected journey time. It is by these routes that the flow $x_{i,k}$ travels and the journey time $y_{i,k} = g_{i,k}(x_{i,k})$ is just sufficient to attract that flow level.

If the shortest journey times $y_{i,k}$ are constructed between all origins i and destinations j, then it follows that

$$x_{ij,k} > 0 \text{ implies } y_{i,k} - y_{j,k} = y_{ij}$$

and

$$y_{i,k} - y_{j,k} < y_{ij} \text{ implies } x_{ij,k} = 0$$

for every load would be carried, in equilibrium, along the shortest time paths. The flow levels will be expected to change until times are equated, and therefore the equilibrium conditions become

$$x_{ij,k} > 0 \text{ implies } g_{i,k}(x_{i,k}) - g_{j,k}(x_{j,k}) = h_{ij}(x_{ij})$$

and

$$g_{i,k}(x_{i,k}) - g_{j,k}(x_{j,k}) < h_{ij}(x_{ij}) \text{ implies } x_{ij,k} = 0$$

for all nodes i and j, and destinations k. The questions about the existence of an equilibrium are therefore really questions about the existence of flow values $x_{ij,k}$ which satisfy these conditions. It is in these terms that the equilibrium will be examined.

A special function was constructed for the general case by M. Beckmann, C. B. Mcguire and C. B. Winsten who not only used it to show the existence of the equilibrium solution but also went further to show that the flow levels x_{ij} along the links are uniquely determined. The function was

$$H(x_{ij,k}; \text{all } i, j \text{ and } k) = \sum_i \sum_k \int_0^{x_{i,k}} g_{i,k}(x) \, dx - \sum_{ij} \int_0^{x_{ij}} h_{ij}(x) \, dx$$

and was arranged so that its first-order partial derivatives resemble parts of the equilibrium conditions,

$$\frac{\delta H}{\delta x_{ij,k}} = g_{i,k}(x_{i,k}) - g_{j,k}(x_{j,k}) - h_{ij}(x_{ij}) \text{ for all } i, j \text{ and } k.$$

A maximum value can be shown to exist for the function in the region $x_{ij,k} \geqslant 0$, all i, j and k, well within the limiting flow levels c_{ij}. Also the function is concave and the Kuhn–Tucker conditions can be applied to the maximum solution. As in the two-route example, they echo the equilibrium conditions and hence show that an equilibrium actually exists for the general network. Moreover, it can be shown that, while the demand and time–flow functions are strictly decreasing and increasing respectively, there will be only one equilibrium set of values for the total flows along the links.

In practice, the optimization property is not usually exploited for actually finding the equilibrium values. A typical situation involves a planning decision in an urban area where it is required to predict how traffic will select actual routes from their origins to destinations. This could, say, help pinpoint possible bottlenecks, or indicate how benefits from investment decisions might be spread through the network. The demand and time–flow functions are hard to evaluate and therefore the function H will be difficult to examine numerically, Instead, computation has been confined to algorithms that attempt directly to mimic the actual vehicle movements. Usually, those used in transportation studies make the assumption that demand is given, and there is adopted a trial-and-error approach of increasing the numbers of journeys along the network links according to their effect on journey time. The time–flow relationships have been variously derived using different functional forms to explain values close to the currently experienced link loadings. A popular example is the exponential function,

$$y_{ij} = k\,e^{cz_{ij}}$$

where the constants k and c are chosen according to present flows and delays. The full procedure starts with an independent assessment of demand levels ready for the 'assignment'. Traffic is added in stages to the road network and the journey times that result used to modify the original hypotheses about demand. The assignment is repeated and demand modified until a reasonable amount of agreement is reached between the demand hypotheses and the conclusions about travel time. This provides the forecast for traffic flows. The discussions here show that there exists an equilibrium solution for which these algorithms can search and indicate some of its properties. In these terms they are important contributions to transport planning.

It is possible now to take up the topic of the efficiency of congestion as a means of rationing road space, and the existence of opportunities for improvement. In other words, the question is asked of whether there is an overall cheaper method of transporting the same loads on the network. In terms of the example, the answer is quickly forthcoming. The allocation to the routes, x_A and x_B, must provide the same total load, i.e.

$$x_A + x_B = x^0,\ x_A,\ x_B \geqslant 0$$

while the smallest value of total cost is sought, total cost being

$$C(x_A, x_B) = h_A(x_A)\,x_A + h_B(x_B)\,x_B$$

Using the method of Lagrange Multipliers (A13) the optimal solution x_A^*, x_B^*, is given by the conditions

$$\frac{\delta C}{\delta x_A} - \lambda \frac{\delta}{\delta x_A}(x_A + x_B) = \frac{\delta C}{\delta x_B} - \lambda \frac{\delta}{\delta x_B}(x_A + x_B) = 0$$

i.e.

$$\frac{\delta C}{\delta x_A} = \frac{\delta C}{\delta x_B}$$

and so

$$x_A^* \frac{dh_A}{dx_A} + h_A(x_A^*) = x_B^* \frac{dh_B}{dx_B} + h_B(x_B^*)$$

If it is assumed that the curves h_A and h_B are the same shape as each other except for the upward shift that is evident in the first diagram in

Fig. 7.4, then this solution will be different to the previous equilibrium point. In terms of the diagram, the equilibrium solution has

$$h_A(x_A^0) = h_B(x_B^0)$$

As

$$x_A^0 \frac{dh_A}{dx_A} > x_B^0 \frac{dh_B}{dx_B}$$

however, the minimum cost solution will have $x_A^* < x_A^0$ and $x_B^* > x_B^0$.
In a more general situation the total transport time–cost is given by

$$\sum_{ij} h_{ij}(x_{ij}) \, x_{ij}$$

As long as the time-flow curve increases at an increasing rate, the total time–cost in convex. If, also, it is supposed that demand is fixed at the equilibrium rate, i.e.

$$\sum_j (x_{ij,k} - x_{ji,k}) = x_{i,k}^0$$

then, from the Kuhn–Tucker conditions with these equality constraints on the non-negative flow values $x_{ij,k}$, it follows that, at the minimum cost solution, x_{ij}^*, $x_{ij,k}^*$,

$$u_{i,k} - u_{j,k} < h_{ij}(x_{ij}^*) + h_{ij}'(x_{ij}^*) \, x_{ij}^* \text{ implies } x_{ij,k}^* = 0$$

and $x_{ij,k}^* > 0$ implies $u_{i,k} - u_{j,k} = h_{ij}(x_{ij}^*) + h_{ij}'(x_{ij}^*) \, x_{ij}^*$ where $u_{i,k}$ are a suitable set of values that play a similar, but not identical, role to the journey times $y_{i,k}$. (h_{ij}' is a short notation for dh_{ij}/dx_{ij}.) By comparison with the equilibrium conditions, the second term, $h_{ij}'(x_{ij}^*) \, x_{ij}^*$, which is added to the congested journey time $h_{ij}(x_{ij}^*)$, represents an extra penalty associated with each link. If this were to be extracted from the operators as an extra levy, the sum of the time–cost and this extra penalty will represent the total effort for carrying a load along each link. The variables $u_{i,k}$ then indicate the effort for travelling from origin i to destination k, and the functions $h_{ij}'(x_{ij}) \, x_{ij}$ evaluate the distortion that distinguishes the equilibrium solution from the optimal cost solution.

The principle of setting extra road tolls to improve the efficiency of the allocation of traffic to routes through the road system has been given serious consideration. A report by the then Ministry of Transport in 1964 on 'road pricing' has outlined the practicalities of metering road vehicles and setting appropriate toll rates. Some points that have not yet been fully investigated, though, are the resulting reorganization of times of travel, the long-term implications about

Traffic Control

travel patterns and the possible inequality of subsequent benefits to the community.

One final remark is worth making about the overall 'best' allocation from the community point of view. The minimum cost solution above was only concerned with demand fixed at the equilibrium level. A global optimum could be constructed to maximize consumer surplus, i.e. the excess of consumer satisfaction over cost. This can be represented by the expression

$$\sum_i \sum_k \int_0^{x_{i,k}} g_{i,k}(x) \, dx - \sum_{ij} h_{ij}(x_{ij}) \, x_{ij}$$

which can be shown to be concave. From the Kuhn–Tucker conditions applied to the optimum $x_{ij,k}{}^+$, $x_{i,k}{}^+$, $x_{ij}{}^+$

$$x_{ij,k}{}^+ > 0 \text{ implies } g_{i,k}(x_{i,k}{}^+) - g_{j,k}(x_{j,k}{}^+) = h_{ij}(x_{ij}{}^+) + h_{ij}{}'(x_{ij}{}^+) \, x_{ij}{}^+$$

and

$$g_{i,k}(x_{i,k}{}^+) - g_{j,k}(x_{j,k}{}^+) = h_{ij}(x_{ij}{}^+) + h_{ij}{}'(x_{ij}{}^+) \, x_{ij}{}^+ \text{ implies } x_{ij,k}{}^+ = 0$$

In this case, the journey times for demand will exceed those actually met en route by an amount $h_{ij}{}'(x_{ij}) \, x_{ij}$. Thus, effectively, the maximum consumer surplus will be obtained when demand is allowed to adjust to a road pricing situation.

7.4 Choice of Time of Travel

The analysis of the last section does not necessarily provide the last word on the efficiency of traffic congestion. It was based on an essentially static queueing model that gave expected journey time as a function of flow and assumed that the road system reached a steady level of flows, steady enough for the expected values to apply. In fact, the actual situations in which traffic networks are heavily loaded are much more likely to have unsteady flow patterns with the loads, or commuters, coming in surges. This would suggest that some acknowledgement of the peak should be incorporated in the model of traffic movement, and also in the attitudes on the demand side to different times of travel. The problem therefore becomes more complicated. To look closer at efficiency for a system that has an element of choice of travel time, the simple example of two routes A and B between two points will again be adopted and used to examine commuter flows between home and workplace.

Suppose that the two routes have uncongested travel times t_A and

t_B and both have the same capacity c. Suppose also that the mechanism of congestion is a straightforward deterministic queue. A flow pattern arrives at the beginning of the road and attempts to move along to the end. When vehicles arrive at a rate greater than the fixed capacity c, however, they have to queue and wait their turn. When the flow recedes, the queue disappears.

To build up a demand model, consider that the decision of when to travel to work comes from a process like that described at the end of chapter 2. There, a commuter's decisions were considered when he was faced with given departure and arrival times for the journey, and valuations were derived in terms of money units for possible alterations. Suppose that the commuters value marginal changes in their departure times at a constant rate, a_1, and in their arrival time at one of two rates a_2 and a_2' according to whether they arrive before or after the appointed time, t', for starting work. If value is accumulated, it will be possible to plot two graphs which together provide the total value of departing and arriving at given times t_1 and t_2, say. These are shown in Fig. 7.5 where the total value, $U(t_1, t_2)$ is given by

$$U(t_1, t_2) = \begin{cases} U + a_1 t_1 - a_2 t_2 & \text{if } t_2 \leqslant t' \\ U + a_1 t_1 - a_2 t' - a_2'(t_2 - t') & \text{otherwise} \end{cases}$$

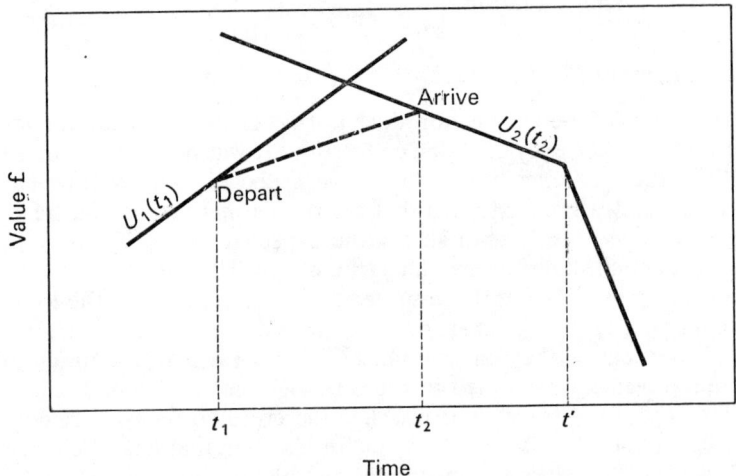

Fig. 7.5 Accumulated value of departing and arriving at t_1 and t_2.

Traffic Control

for some constant, U. It is assumed that all commuters are sufficiently alike to have the same positive values for the trade-off rates, a_1, a_2 and a_2' which satisfy the ranking $a_2 > a_1 > a_2'$, and that each commuter attempts to choose his travel time to give himself the highest value possible.

If there were no congestion on either route from home to workplace, it would be possible to find the value that a commuter places on leaving at any particular time t by substituting $t_2 = t + t_A$ or $t_2 = t + t_B$ in the above expression. For route A

$$U(t, t + t_A) = \begin{cases} U - a_2 t_A + (a_1 - a_2)t & \text{if } t \leqslant t' - t_A \\ U - (a_2 - a_2')t' - a_2' t_A + (a_1 - a_2')t, & \text{otherwise} \end{cases}$$

and similarly for route B. It will rise and fall for each route as time t is increased and have maximum points when $t = t' - t_A$ for route A and $t = t' - t_B$ for route B. As it is assumed that $t_A < t_B$, the largest value overall will be obtained by travelling along route A, departing at time $t = t' - t_A$. If everyone attempts to take advantage of this time, they will not be able to all move along the route within the fixed capacity. Therefore, while some commuters travel at this time, accepting the possible queue, others will be prepared to shift to other times when there is a smaller queue. An equilibrium flow pattern would be expected as commuters shift to level off the advantages of travelling at any particular time.

To find the equilibrium it is necessary to search for a flow pattern in which the total value obtained by commuters actually travelling is the same whatever their time of departure and route, and the value for other times is less. In other words, if the departure flows along the two routes are $x_A(t)$ and $x_B(t)$ for departure time t, and vehicles leaving at that time experience queue lengths of $t_A(t)$ and $t_B(t)$, then the equilibrium conditions are as follows,

$$x_A(t) > 0 \text{ implies } U(t, t + t_A(t)) = U^0$$
$$x_B(t) > 0 \text{ implies } U(t, t + t_B(t)) = U^0$$
$$U(t, t + t_A(t)) < U^0 \text{ implies } x_A(t) = 0$$

and

$$U(t, t + t_B(t)) < U^0 \text{ implies } x_B(t) = 0$$

where U^0 is the largest value ever experienced. The only pattern that meets the conditions is shown in Fig. 7.6. At a time when the value of travelling along an uncongested route A is exactly U^0, i.e.

$$U - a_2 t_A + (a_1 - a_2) t_1^A = U^0$$

the flow begins along route A and increases sufficiently quickly to increase the queue length at the rate $(a_2 - a_1)/a_1$ so that the value, U,

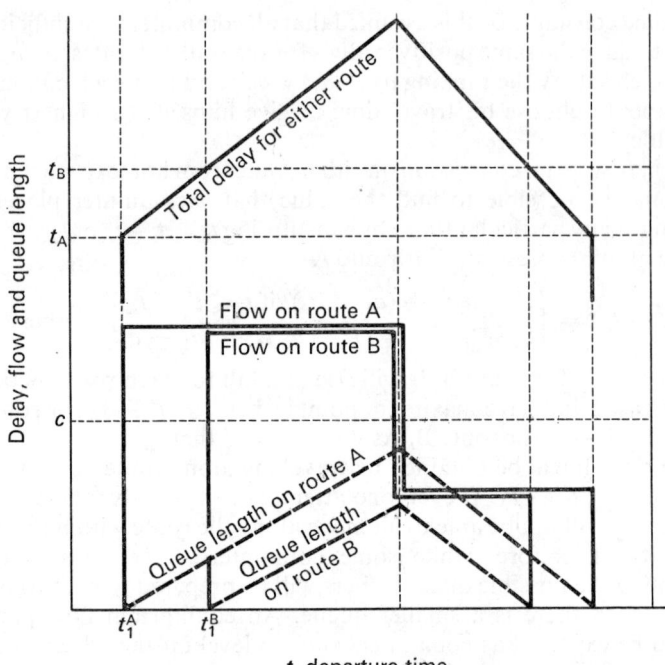

Fig. 7.6 The equilibrium pattern for delays, flows and queue lengths for the two routes A and B.

again remains constant. Eventually, when the queue length becomes zero, the flow ceases. The pattern along route B will behave similarly but entirely independently.

This model gives a different allocation to routes A and B from the last one. For the particular example, it provides another answer to the question of efficiency of the split between the routes. The outflow from each route will be constant, while the commuters are travelling. Therefore, if the departure times were rearranged to give a steady inflow at rate c, there would be no congestion, and hence a minimum time–cost allocation would be achieved. The interesting point is that the numbers travelling would not change. So the actual total distribution to the routes in the equilibrium will be the same as for the optimal transport cost, and it is only the journey times that are changed. In this respect, with the new model and the particular example, the congested distribution is efficient! So it would appear that no travellers should be discouraged from travelling on the route of their choice by a route toll. Rather the times of travel should be readjusted.

8 Models of Location

The last chapter concentrated on the complications that have to be considered when congestion becomes a major determinant of the distribution pattern. It was a very narrow examination of traffic problems within a transport system. Now the questions are broadened to the other extreme, and look at the problems of planning location when transport costs play a major part. Setting aside possible variations due to availability of natural resources, the cost of moving goods and people about is the way that a planner becomes aware of the geography of an area. In fact, it could be said that in the long term, when it is possible to ignore the locational advantages that arise through the past development of facilities, the test of economic efficiency of the layout of an area lies with the size and distribution of the transport costs. Mathematical programming helps find an optimal layout with respect to these costs, and, at the same time, indicates equilibrium patterns for the location of economic activities. This aspect will be expanded in this chapter.

In this context, the two approaches that were mentioned earlier, normative and positive, are closely related. At the outset the first attempts to use the underlying model to examine policy objectives, while the second uses it to explain current patterns and predict into the future. As has been seen, though, when discussing the behaviour of firms, if the market has a strong element of perfect competition, the distinction becomes blurred. Previously, the same result was obtained whether optimization was carried out over the whole industry or simply within individual profit-maximizing firms which operate under competition. The following models are based on a similar joint approach. They each centre around a single optimization problem specified in terms of the whole area, but the interest lies in the properties of the optimal solution when interpreted in terms of the individual economic organizations. The optimization problems in each case are developed on the basis of costs and rents derived from the transportation problem.

8.1 Location and Economic Rent

Suppose that the basic transportation problem is applied to a firm with both depots and customers at each of the points i, $i = 1, \ldots n$ and that it involves a transport network where the cost of carrying a unit of the firm's product from depot D_i to customer C_j is c_{ij}. Suppose also that the actual production costs, and hence the minimum price at which the firm will sell its product at the depots, is independent of location and denoted by c. Similarly, the value of goods to all the customers is the same and is denoted by p, the greatest price at which they will buy. The transport costs can then each be replaced by the net revenue, $r_{ij} = p - c - c_{ij}$, gained from taking a unit of product from depot D_i and selling it to customer C_j. If there are x_{ij} such units, $i, j = 1, \ldots n$, then the total net revenue will be

$$\sum_{i=1}^{n} \sum_{j=1}^{n} r_{ij} x_{ij}$$

and, if the available quantities at the depots and requirements by the customers are d_i and c_j respectively, then a profit-maximizing firm would be expected to seek maximum net revenue subject to the constraints

$$\sum_{j=1}^{n} x_{ij} = d_i, i = 1, \ldots n$$

and

$$\sum_{i=1}^{n} x_{ij} = c_j, j = 1, \ldots n$$

where

$$x_{ij} \geq 0, i, j = 1, \ldots n$$

By treating the problem as one where negated net revenue is minimized, two sets of shadow costs u_i^0 and v_j^0, $i, j = 1, \ldots n$, can be attached to the optimal solution. They would be such that

$$u_i^0 + v_j^0 < -r_{ij} = -(p - c - c_{ij}) \text{ implies } x_{ij}^0 = 0$$

and

$$x_{ij}^0 > 0 \text{ implies } u_i^0 + v_j^0 = -r_{ij} = -(p - c - c_{ij}).$$

In other words, the sum of the shadow costs for a depot/customer pair between which goods are transported is equal to the negated marginal profit when an extra unit is carried.

Firms operating in the long term would be expected to adjust their operation until the profitability at the margin and in total is zero. For this to happen the costs and selling prices must be made equal to

Models of Location

$(c - u_i^0)$ and $(p + v_j^0)$ and so must trace out a cost 'surface' and a price 'surface' that would apply to a long-term equilibrium. It remains to see whether a suitable adjustment mechanism can be found.

One possible situation could involve the firms increasing their profit by adjusting the levels of supply and modifying their selection of customers. So, if the marginal profitability were not zero, the changing returns to scale in the production processes and the varying attitudes of the customers to price would eventually lead to a long-term equilibrium where profit is maximized. Then, the actual costs at the depots and prices to the customers follow the surfaces mentioned above and the shadow costs at the new optimum will total to zero.

A second situation, and one that is more interesting, is that the firms stick to their depot and customer levels either as a matter of policy, or because of circumstances outside their control. Then, with competition both within and outside the industry for goods used in the firms' own and their customers' production processes, the locational advantages will be eaten away. The most common factor of production at each point is land. Given that there is sufficient land available at each location for the depots and customers, then the firms or their customers will be prepared to spend, in the absence of other locational factors, up to the amounts $-u_i^0$ and $-v_j^0$, respectively on rent for that land in the face of other possible users. The negated shadow costs, therefore, can be interpreted as *economic rents*, the maximum amounts chargeable for locating depot or customer facilities at particular points. Hence, while conditions of perfect competition exist in the land market, the price and cost surface coincides with the pattern of market rents appropriate to unit levels of each kind of activity. On the other hand, if the depots or customers dominated the land market at certain locations, it would only be possible to equate negated shadow costs with the rent of marginal pieces of land required for possible changes in the quota transported to or from these points. Then the complete pattern of rents observed over the area might be quite different.

Another way to look at the rent surface is to consider a global landlord extracting rents $-u_i$ and $-v_j$ from the firms and their customers. Whereas the first problem, the primal, concentrated on maximizing the amount of profit obtained by the firm, a second and related problem, the dual, attempts to minimize the total rent obtained by the landlord, i.e. minimize

$$-\sum_{i=1}^{n} d_i u_i - \sum_{j=1}^{n} c_j v_j$$

subject to

$$u_i + v_j \leqslant c_{ij} + c - p$$

These dual constraints ensure that any locational advantage is absorbed in rent charges. The same shadow cost values u_i^0, v_j^0, provide the optimum in the dual as well as being associated with the optimum in the primal. Also the two objective function values are equal in the optimum. Therefore, it would appear that a landlord who was forced to accept the smallest total rent would still drain away all the tenants' profits, the optimal rent bill being equal to the optimal profit. So, if the land market is a perfectly competitive one and the tenants are successful in paying as little as possible for their land, the total profit to the firm, net of rent, will be zero.

Finally, it is worth mentioning two interpretations that can be placed on shadow costs when they do not actually represent the rents themselves. Firstly, suppose that a firm which is close to its long-term equilibrium distribution were observed to choose its depot and customer quotas equal to d_i and c_j. It would then be acting as though its location rents were given by the values $-u_i^0$ and $-v_j^0$, even if they were not. They would represent the apparent perfectly competitive prices of the land for a firm which could well be in an imperfect position. Secondly, consider that it is required, as part of a central plan, to encourage the firm to adopt a distribution pattern with totals d_i and c_j. If it operated under conditions of perfect competition, then the imposition of the rent pattern $-u_i^0$, $-v_j^0$ would encourage it to choose to transport goods between the same depot and customer pairs as in the optimal solution of the above primal problem. By this choice the firm would make a zero profit instead of a negative one for other pairs. Further, amongst the different combinations of the amounts of goods transported between each pair, there will be the required pattern d_i, c_j, and therefore, since the firm would be expected to be indifferent between the combinations, it could be persuaded to adopt exactly the required levels of production and supply. Moreover, the negated shadow costs provide the only artificial sets of rents which could help to implement such a locational policy. To impose the required pattern under the conditions of perfect competition, the land would have to be bought and sold by the controlling body until rents met the required levels. The distribution of transport activities could then be allowed to follow as a result of the mechanism of the market itself.

8.2 The Location of Industrial Activity within a Region

A model that has been proposed by B. H. Stevens and E. W. Coughlin attempts to examine the location of industrial activity and the associated flows of goods within a metropolitan region. It is intended as an

Models of Location

aid to planners looking at alterations in land-use patterns over a period of 15 to 20 years, and assumes that one goal amongst their objectives is the attainment of economic efficiency through the 'minimum utilization of transportation'. This would be expected to arise if the various economic markets operated under perfect competition. It is doubtful, though, that they do, and the model can pretend to be little more than a normative tool, serving as a means of formulating the initial proposal for a planning policy.

It is assumed that reasonable estimates can be made for a large variety of economic data. The region is broken into m sub-areas for which the present land-usage is known in detail, down to a breakdown by industrial activities. In addition, projections of consumer demand are taken to the target date for goods produced in each of the n industries, and an assessment is made of the total imports and exports of the region to other regions that make up the national picture.

The minimization of transport costs is undertaken with restrictions placed on the variables, the levels of activity and flows between the sub-areas. There are four types of constraint. Firstly, the *land constraints* point to the limited availability of land within any area at the future date. In this case, it is only industrial land that is considered, other land-uses somewhat unrealistically remaining constant throughout the model. The amount of land is calculated on the basis of current figures and modified by changes that it is anticipated will be permitted by the planning authorities in their initial structuring. These may be revised as a result of the examination of the solution to the model. Secondly, *consumption constraints* ensure that consumer demand is satisfied in each area by the surplus of each good left over from the total quantities that are produced and imported after industry has itself consumed the good and other quantities have been exported. Thirdly, the *quota constraints* set the standards required by inter-regional trade. The total shipments of commodities in and out of the region must meet the projected levels. Finally, the *output constraints* are added to recognize the investment in industrial activity evident in the current land-use pattern. As such, a minimum level of production is fixed for the future output in each sub-area. The model therefore allocates only the new production activities beyond those presently established, and does not attempt to restructure beyond the output constraints. The minimum output levels may, however, be revalued once the first solution is known.

The model can be formally phrased in terms of non-negative variables $x_k{}^l$ which generally refer to the levels of outputs of industry k in sub-area l measured in terms of units of product k, and the variables ${}^l s_i{}^l$ which are the levels of shipment of good i from sub-areas

j to l. The overall aim is to minimize transportation costs within the region, i.e. minimize

$$\sum_{i=1}^{n} \sum_{j=1}^{m} \sum_{l=1}^{m} {}^{j}c_i^{l} \, {}^{j}s_i^{l}$$

where the coefficients ${}^{j}c_i^{l}$ are the costs of transporting a unit of good i between sub-areas j and l. The summations involve transport costs between all pairs of sub-areas for all commodities.

The optimization is subjected to the following constraints:
(a) Land constraints,

$$\sum_{k=1}^{n} a_k x_k^{l} \leqslant R^l, l = 1, \ldots m$$

where a_k is the fixed number of units of industrial land needed per unit output of good k, and R^l is the number of units of industrial land available in sub-area l. This sets an upper limit on the total amount of land used in an area for production.

(b) Consumption constraints,

$$x_i^{l} + \sum_{j=1}^{m} {}^{j}s_i^{l} - \sum_{j=1}^{m} {}^{l}s_i^{j} - \sum_{k=1}^{n} {}_ib_k x_k^{l} \geqslant D_i^{l}, l = 1, \ldots m, i = 1, \ldots n$$

where ${}_ib_k$ is the fixed number of units of good i needed as input per unit output of good k, an D_i^{l} is the projected consumer demand for good i in sub-area l. Hence the level of production of a good enhanced by the shipments of the good into the sub-area exceeds the amounts shipped out and consumed in production of all other goods by at least the consumer demand.

(c) Quota constraints,

$$\sum_{j=1}^{m} {}^{j}s_i^{w} = Q_i^{w}, i = 1, \ldots n$$

and

$$\sum_{j=1}^{m} {}^{w}s_i^{j} = {}^{w}Q_i, i = 1, \ldots n$$

where ${}^{j}s_i^{w}$ and ${}^{w}s_i^{j}$ are shipments of good i to and from a dummy area w in which all the inter-regional and national transport terminals are situated, and ${}^{w}Q_i$, Q_i^{w} are the import and export quotas for the region as a whole. The projected levels of participation in inter-regional trade must be attained.

Models of Location

(d) Output constraints,

$$x_k^l \geqslant O_k^l, l = 1, \ldots m, k = 1, \ldots n$$

where O_k^l is the minimum output level for production activity k in sub-area l.

The optimization will be carried out with all the constraints in operation. It may be required to look at the solution and revise certain constant values, as, for example, when sub-areas in which all available land is used are recognized as 'central' areas. If the social costs of traffic congestion and demolition were not too great, these areas could well be developed further, beyond the previously established limit, and hence the land constraint constants relaxed. Otherwise, a new policy could improve access to 'non-central' areas by additional investment in the transport system, in which case the coefficients ${}^j c_i^l$ would be modified. The final optimal solution provides estimates for the levels of industrial and associated activities, e.g. warehousing, and hence some plans could be drawn up for the facilities and employment that would then be required. Thus a prediction of intra-regional flows of goods including commuter flows could be obtained alongside the optimal plan.

In all, the solution will provide a detailed description of a situation where transport costs are minimized. There are many weak points in the formulation, but the proponents suggest that with extreme caution the model can give helpful advice in planning problems.

8.3 Distribution of Residential Activity

A different model has been postulated by J. D. Herbert and B. H. Stevens to distribute residential activity for the Penn–Jersey Transportation Study. It is part of a larger scheme designed to locate all types of land-using activity in an urban area, and attempts to distribute in an optimal pattern a 'wave' of new households generated within a time period of about a year. They are placed on residential land whose locational attributes are already established through the existing land-use pattern. The numbers of households involved and the amount of land available is supposed already forecast independently and descriptive information is assumed readily available about the actual households and the transportation system. (This particular model was to be applied alongside a comprehensive transportation survey.)

Household behaviour models are necessarily much more complex in their descriptions of locational choice than those explaining industrial patterns. This model is no exception and has a detailed structure to the decision processes built around the observed expenditure of different types of household. Basically, the total budget is assumed split between (*a*) house maintenance costs, (*b*) site rent for a house located at a specific point in the area (or equivalent rent in the case of interest paid for land purchase), (*c*) travel costs associated with the requirements of that household and expressed as the number of trips for different categories of purpose, and (*d*) expenditure on all other goods bought by the household. As a result, satisfaction is gained from (i) the house, (ii) the amount of land on which it is sited, (iii) the amenity level attributed to the location, and (iv) the other goods purchased.

The operational basis for the model relies on the assumption that, at the present time, large numbers of households of similar types have already located so as to achieve optimal levels of satisfaction. It would then be possible to construct indifference sets for each type of household for 'market baskets', i.e. combinations of house, site of a particular size, amenity level and 'bundle' of other commodities, among which the households would reach the same level of satisfaction. The market baskets will vary over locations, as will their cost through differences in house construction and travel patterns. In particular, the travel costs will be made up from a combination of the specific location and household trip requirements. This will enable origins and destinations to be designated and trip costs collected into the total travel budget. Another cost that varies with location is site rent but, for the moment, it is left out of the budget. The remaining costs, such as the purchase of other goods, will not vary with the position of the house but may, of course, still differ between household types. In summary, the household will make a choice between locations, and hence market baskets, knowing that for every possible position for its house there will be a total cost which, for the moment, is exclusive of site rent.

For every location there can be said to be a 'saving' resulting from the difference between the total household budget and the budget net of site rent. The assumption of the model is that the choice of location will be the one which maximizes the household's savings. There are two ways in which this might come about. The first assumes that landlords are in a strong bargaining position and are able to extract the largest returns. The second is where not all the advantages of the site are consumed in rent, but there is an opportunity to gain extra satisfaction from spare income. In both cases the incentive would be expected to be to maximize savings.

An equilibrium point that could be reached is one where total savings for all individuals together are maximized. Then, no person can oust another from a particular location, for otherwise there would be a drop in total savings and the new entry at a location would be bidding less than the person he had removed. The solution of maximum

Models of Location

aggregate savings also brings up again a community goal mentioned in the last chapter. If all land were supplied free, donated, say, by a mythical socialist state (or otherwise provided at a constant rent), the optimization would effectively be the maximization of consumer surplus. Hence not only does the exercise have a predictive content, it also has a direct interpretation in the sense of social welfare.

The formulation of the problem is refreshingly simple, the complexities being left to the evaluation of the constants. Altogether there are p sub-areas for location choice and m market baskets to choose from in each of the n household groups. The allocation made by a household of group i to the purchase of market basket h is denoted by b_{ih}, and the actual cost for location in sub-area k by c_{ih}^k. Also s_{ih} is used as the number of acres in the site occupied by a household of group i if it chooses market basket h. Therefore, where x_{ih}^k is the non-negative number of households of group i using market basket h in sub-area k, the problem is to maximize

$$z \equiv \sum_{k=1}^{p} \sum_{i=1}^{n} \sum_{h=1}^{m} (b_{ih} - c_{ih}^k) x_{ih}^k$$

subject to

$$\sum_{i=1}^{n} \sum_{h=1}^{m} s_{ih} x_{ih}^k \leqslant L^k, k = 1, \ldots p$$

and

$$\sum_{k=1}^{p} \sum_{h=1}^{m} x_{ih}^k = N_i, i = 1, \ldots n$$

where there are L^k acres available for residential use for a particular year's allocation in sub-area k, and N_i households to be distributed in group i. Of the constraints, the first set prevent the consumption of land in each sub-area from exceeding the land available. The second set ensure that the required number of households are located. As long as there is more than a minimum amount of land, an optimal solution will exist.

The dual problem is capable of interpretation in terms of an overall renting policy. In contrast with the primal problem which optimizes aggregate rent-paying ability, it minimizes total land rent collected by the rentier class net of subsidies. A statement of this problem is to minimize

$$z' \equiv \sum_{k=1}^{p} L^k r^k + \sum_{i=1}^{n} N_i v_i$$

subject to

$$s_{ih}r^k + v_i \geqslant b_{ih} - c_{ih}{}^k, k = 1, \ldots p, i = 1, \ldots n, h = 1, \ldots m$$

where only the variables r^k, which represent the rents per unit of land in sub-area k, are non-negative. They will take positive values in the optimal solution when an area is fully occupied by households and indicate the level to which bidding must go to secure the land for those who live there. For such households the rent values will be equal to or less than the smallest savings in the sub-area. The variables v_i take on both positive and negative values, and can be interpreted as subsidies or taxes which could be imposed by the central planning authority. They either increase the budget of those who, because of low bidding ability, would not otherwise be able to find any houses at all, or, alternatively, to take away some advantage from those groups with high bidding abilities who do not occupy as much land as they could if there were greater numbers of them.

Although the model establishes a rent surface for the whole area, there is a significant point brought out in the original paper. The model is sensitive in the eventual pattern of rents to the degree of aggregation in the description of household groups and areas of land. Broadly speaking, the finer the breakdown of areas and the coarser the household groups, the less will be the emphasis on the subsidy variables v_i, for there will be more households which are located on sites with one type only. As the limit is approached, the variable virtually disappears altogether, and the model is reduced more and more to a continuous one with rent as the only significant dual variable on sites that are occupied. Thus the linear programming problem allows an approximation to be made to what is, from the point of view of computation, a difficult continuous formulation.

There are a number of problems in the application of the model. Briefly, besides the normal difficulties surrounding collection of data and forecasting, they arise through the restriction of household choice to a single indifference set, the optimization over single yearly steps and possible interactions between households locating near each other that may arise from, say, the competition for jobs in a particular area. To allow for these difficulties inevitably involves complicating the model by introducing more factors or otherwise bringing in non-linearities. As it stands, though, it provides a basis for making policy decisions about such areas of public interest as 'zoning', transportation, redevelopment and public housing, and, although there are other considerations, particularly in the field of social welfare, it still provides an indication of what happens if there is a move away from the narrow objectives used here.

8.4 A Model of Industrial Location and Trade between Regions

The search for optimum location patterns can be extended from the intra- to inter-regional level. Locational advantages at the regional level determine to a considerable extent the specializations in particular industries. A model developed by L. Moses was used specifically to investigate the connection between inter-regional trade and the location of economic activity throughout the United States. As is pointed out in his paper, however, it could similarly be applied to most other groupings of regions for which cost of transfer of goods is a significant factor in determining the amount of trade.

The model can be described by considering r regions ($p = 1, \ldots r$), within which the economic activities involve the production and distribution of m homogenous goods and services ($i = 1, \ldots m$). Each firm is supposed to produce a single product which, once classified, is a perfect substitute for the products of the same category produced in different regions. It is possible, however, for the technology of firms with the same product to vary amongst regions. There is a single transport medium available and a household sector that provides a labour input to production.

The required data involves regional demands for goods and the capacity and technology of production. There will be mr final demands Y_i^p to determine, Y_i^p being the number of units of good i demanded by a household in region p. Also there are limits to the amount of activity that can take place in any area. K_i^p is the total productive capacity of all firms that produce good i, K_t^p is the maximum amount of freight than can be handled by the transport industry in a given period of time, and L^p is the maximum amount of labour supplied by households, all in area p. There is no subscript on the labour capacity, for the model assumes that within each region labour is homogeneous and perfectly mobile. Labour is not able, though, to move across regional boundaries. Finally, there needs to be specified the activity table for each region, to indicate the inputs required for unit levels of the producing and transporting activities. In the latter case, because of the diverse nature of the loads, separate activities are created for each good carried. So a_{ij}^p is the amount of good i required to produce a unit of good j in region p, and ${}_iv_j^{pq}$ is the amount of good i required in region p to transport good j from region p to q. Inputs to the transport industry are assumed to be acquired at the origin end of the journey.

With the help of this information the model is able to determine directly the optimal pattern of inter-regional and intra-regional shipments described by the non-negative variables s_i^{pq} which indicate the amount of good i transported from region p to q. The solution then indirectly gives the optimal regional outputs for each good, i.e.

$$x_i^p = \sum_{q=1}^{r} s_i^{pq},$$

the national outputs and a breakdown of transportation costs obtained by multiplying total shipments by the relevant money shipping costs. The optimum is defined by the minimum total transport cost chosen from different regional purchase patterns for the producing industries and households. There are no money costs entering directly into the data (other than the use of money values to define quantities of goods) and, as the only input bought outside the system is labour, the labour costs are the only ones entering the objective function. It is therefore required to minimize

$$z \equiv \sum_{i=1}^{m} \sum_{p=1}^{r} \sum_{q=1}^{r} (a_{li}^p + {}_iv_i^{pq}) s_i^{pq}$$

where a_{li}^p and ${}_iv_i^{pq}$ are the labour inputs in production and transportation respectively.

The constraints on variables s_i^{pq} arise from the inventories of goods within a region and the upper limits on production, transportation and household activities. In the first instance, of the goods that are produced in and imported to a region, some are exported, some are used in the production of other goods and the remainder consumed by the household sector. The total amount of good i in region p will therefore be given by

$$x_i^p + \sum_{\substack{q=1 \\ q \neq p}}^{r} s_i^{qp} = \sum_{q=1}^{r} (s_i^{pq} + s_i^{qp}) - s_i^{pp}$$

This will be distributed according to the breakdown of exports, inputs for production and household demand, i.e.

$$\sum_{\substack{q=1 \\ q \neq p}}^{r} s_i^{pq} + \left(\sum_{j=1}^{m} a_{ij}^p x_j^p + \sum_{j=1}^{m} \sum_{q=1}^{r} {}_iv_j^{pq} s_j^{pq} \right) + Y_i^p$$

Therefore, on equating both sides

$$\sum_{q=1}^{r} (s_i^{pq} + s_i^{qp}) = \sum_{q=1}^{r} s_i^{pq} + \sum_{j=1}^{m} \sum_{q=1}^{r} (a_{ij}^p + {}_iv_j^{pq}) s_j^{pq} + Y_i^p$$

i.e.

$$\sum_{q=1}^{r} s_i^{qp} - \sum_{j=1}^{m} \sum_{q=1}^{r} (a_{ij}^p + {}_iv_j^{pq}) s_j^{pq} = Y_i^p, \ i=1, \ldots m, \ p=1, \ldots r.$$

Some additional constraints are necessary to ensure that production does not outstep its capacity limits,

i.e. $$x_i^p = \sum_{q=1}^{r} s_i^{pq} \leqslant K_i^p, i = 1, \ldots m, p = 1, \ldots r,$$

that transportation, with the varying use by different goods of capital equipment indicated by the weights $w_i^p, p = 1, \ldots r, i = 1, \ldots m$, does not exceed a maximum level,

i.e. $$\sum_{i=1}^{m} \sum_{q=1}^{r} w_i^p s_i^{pq} \leqslant K_t^p, p = 1, \ldots r$$

and, finally, that not more than a maximum level of labour input is used in total in a region,

i.e. $$\sum_{i=1}^{m} \sum_{q=1}^{r} (a_{1i}^p + {}_iv_i^{pq}) s_i^{pq} \leqslant L^p, p = 1, \ldots r.$$

In the application to trade in the United States the formulation of the model was amended to cater for some of the realities of the situation. Foreign trade was determined outside the model, and exports introduced through increased demand in the regions containing ports. On the other hand, imports were included by setting up fictitious 'import' industries with no factor inputs. Also, because of lack of data, all shipment costs were calculated on the basis of rail transport and, because of difficulties in description, the service industries were excluded from the optimization leaving only manufacturing industries. Inputs were still included for the excluded activities, but their pattern of operation was determined outside the model. Further, it was recognized that inaccuracies would occur through too much aggregation in the definition of regions and industries. Coarse classifications cause errors to arise in the amount of transportation usage through the distinction between inter- and intra-regional shipments, and also allow a great deal of substitution between goods produced within an industry. As a result, it is preferable to include as many industries and regions as it is possible to manipulate in the calculations. The number of constraints and variables increases rapidly with an increasingly fine breakdown and a special method of solution was developed. This used a combination of the techniques developed for the transportation problem and input–output analysis which is described in the next chapter, and it is claimed that it could cope with as many as 450 industries and 100 regions.

The model was used mainly to explain the patterns of trade at the time for which the data applied. It traced foreign imports and exports through to consumption by households, and consumption and production by industries, and therefore determined the reliance placed by each region on the economic development of foreign countries. Equally, internal domestic trade balances could be constructed to indicate the comparative advantages achieved through location. In relation to this, the transportation costs were dropped out of the model for one calculation so that the effect of costs of moving goods could be appreciated.

9 Linear Techniques and the Economy

The author so far has developed the ideas of activity analysis from single firms to industries, urban areas and collections of regions. The final step is to look at the possibility of modelling the whole economy, at least from the point of view of production. The aim will be to examine what many would claim is the most fundamental problem of economics, how national resources can be best employed.

At this level, the scale of the numerical side of the problem is large. Of course, the economy is an extremely complex system and difficulties of definition of activities, problems of data acquisition and shear size of a full activity table prohibit the straightforward extension of the optimization techniques mentioned earlier. Nevertheless, mathematical programming has been shown to be useful on at least two important fronts. Firstly, the algebraic formulations enable a considerable amount of theoretical housekeeping to be carried out on the existence and characteristics of competitive equilibria and welfare criteria. This in itself helps to establish some principles of national planning. Secondly, by making appropriate simplifications to the structure of the economy it is possible to move from statements of national accounts to a quantitative model that can both indicate how future targets might be met, and also how specific quantities might be affected by policy changes. In this way it is possible to find sufficient data to build up a useful activity table.

9.1 A Complete Productive System

Before developing the two applications of mathematical programming, consider the extent of the problem. The productive economy is simply a collection of firms and industries of the type discussed in Chapter 5. Its technology could therefore be described in one large activity table in which productive activities and goods are listed, and the coefficients a_{ij} indicate the amount of good i that is employed in or produced by the operation of activity j at unit level. Thus, if the activities were used at levels x_j, the total amount of good i required or produced in the economy as a whole will be

$$y_i = \sum_j a_{ij} x_j$$

These totals mark the transition between micro-economics and macro-economics. Whereas the coefficients a_{ij} are framed in terms of the operation of industries which are collections of individual firms, the totals y_i indicate the position of the economy as a whole, and the values they take play a significant part in framing national policy. As a result, the levels x_j represent a means to an end; they describe the actual production plan that, if enforced by appropriate action within the industries, will achieve the targets y_i.

An assumption that has again slipped into the argument is of constant returns to scale in the production processes. There was some discussion of the alternatives in earlier chapters. Now it will almost always be an acceptable assumption for small changes in the activity levels when the coefficients are interpreted at the margins, but when shifts are larger, as might occur when plans are drawn up involving drastic alterations, some variation would be accepted. These points were first generally discussed by the French–Swiss economist L. Walras in the latter half of the nineteenth century, when it was remarked that there are two consolations. Firstly, the modeller is free to choose the level of aggregation at which the production activities are introduced. Thus, even though the production functions of individual firms are not linear, the representation of the industry could well be. So the formulation would be concerned with the level of output of the industry without necessarily bothering about the allocation between individual firms. Secondly, as long as there is some mechanism for industrial management decisions, such as the choice of activities in a profit-maximizing firm, the variation of coefficients can be represented by the inclusion of a number of alternative production processes all with constant coefficients. Then, instead of varying the coefficients in one process, the mechanism would change the process itself to one with different valued coefficients.

The activity table formulation allows a comprehensive examination of modern production. With the advancement of technology it has become possible, especially in the petroleum and chemical industries, to establish firms whose processes result in a large number of goods being jointly produced. In fact, the outputs and inputs to different processes are often related in complex chains of dependence. In the activity table the categorization of goods into inputs and outputs is left to the sign of the coefficients a_{ij}. Historically this has not been the way goods have been treated, and there has been much more emphasis on

Linear Techniques and the Economy

dividing them into the groups *primary*, *intermediate* and *final*. The first indicates those materials which are provided by nature from the land or from human sources, and which are essentially inputs to the system. Recently it has become fashionable to think in terms of 'resources' rather than 'primary factors', and to expand the list that once centred on land and labour to include supplies of fuel and minerals. Intermediate goods are those that are both produced and consumed by the system as part of production, and the final products are the outputs of the whole productive system that are 'creamed off' to be consumed in another sector of the economy. The final result of allocating the input quantitites $-y_i$ of primary goods i is therefore the output y_i of final goods i, while the intermediate goods appear and disappear within the system. Thus the production plan $x_j, j = 1, \ldots n$, indicates a strategy by which national resources can be employed to move towards the consumption goals $y_i, i = 1, \ldots m$, of society.

As has been mentioned earlier, the complexity of the problems requires the incorporation of a number of simplifying assumptions. In the two approaches that follow the issues revolve around the inclusion in the models of (*a*) joint production, (*b*) alternative production processes, and (*c*) the division of goods into the three traditional categories. By adhering to some restrictive assumptions, the theoretical points are manageable within the linear programming framework, and the concepts quite easily understood. The theory does not necessarily collapse on introducing developments but it does become more blurred. Therefore, whilst admitting the need in modern studies for as general a set of formulations as possible, the excuse is made here that this chapter is intended as an introduction to further studies, and the simplifying assumptions will be introduced where they make the going easier.

9.2 Perfectly Competitive Equilibrium

Following the earlier discussions of perfect competition, particularly in Chapters 5 and 8, it is interesting to look at the theoretical significance for the whole economy. For this purpose the formulation that will be described is the one that has become known as the *Walras–Cassel System of general equilibrium*, named as it is after Walras and his early twentieth century 'popularizer', G. Cassel. It assumes that there are no intermediate goods, and that there are n activities j solely concerned with the production of n products j. a_{ij} is the fixed amount of resource $i, i = 1, \ldots m$, required in unit production of product j and, because of the split into resources and products, they will be non-negative. The goods involved are bought and sold in perfectly competitive markets where information about prices is rapidly transmitted. The point of interest is whether, in the ideal world of the model, a set of non-negative values can be found for prices which will allow an allocation of resources to the production processes that makes sense in terms of a perfectly competitive equilibrium. For this, the profitability of each activity must be zero, the consumer demand for final products satisfied at the level appropriate for current prices, and the supply of resources ensured by the current price of supply. More precisely, the questions asked concern the existence of a solution to the equation system describing the equilibrium and, moreover, they examine the nature of its properties. Although these are two academic points in themselves, if satisfactory answers can be found, then they will mean that there is a consistent system which can be laid behind the observations of the real world. This would be an important foundation stone for any subsequent analysis.

To look at the detail of the model, assume that the prices of products and resources are denoted by the non-negative variables $p_j, j = 1, \ldots n$, and $q_i, i = 1, \ldots m$ respectively. It would then be possible to describe consumer demand by the functions $f_j(p_1 \ldots p_n, y), j = 1, \ldots n$ where y is some parameter describing income. These functions could be derived by gathering together individual decisions made on the basis of personal optimizations in the light of prices $p_1 \ldots p_n$ and income y. What is perhaps more relevant from the point of view of this model is that income will be determined by some mechanism involving consideration of prices in general, both from the resource and product sides. Therefore a more appropriate representation of consumer demand is a set of functions $f_j(p_1 \ldots p_n, q_1 \ldots q_m), j = 1, \ldots n$. Similarly, to cope with the most general cases of resources being extracted from human and natural resources, the supply functions could be constructed to indicate exactly how much of factor j would be available for each set of prices. Here a simplifying assumption will be made, however, and resource supplies will be taken as fixed at levels $r_i, i = 1, \ldots m$.

The demand and supply relationships represent a description of external requirements on the economy. Obviously, in any system of equilibrium, demand must be satisfied and supply be adequate. In terms of the activity table this means that, for the equilibrium set of prices,

$$x_j = f_j(p_1 \ldots p_n, q_1 \ldots q_m), j = 1, \ldots n$$

$$\sum_{j=1}^{n} a_{ij} x_j \leqslant r_i, i = 1, \ldots m$$

The first set of equations could be expressed as a set of inequalities and thus allow for the possibility of surplus products. If the associated producing activities are cut back, however, then, without loss of generality, the constraints would be exactly met. At the other end of the processes, it is quite possible for there to be surplus supply of some resource i. If this were to happen in the equilibrium, then it would be expected that, after competitive bidding in the markets, the price would be zero. Similarly, as competitive systems are supposed to eat away the profit on all operational activities, the balance for each activity of income to outgoings must be less than or equal to zero. Hence, for all production activities j,

$$\sum_{i=1}^{m} a_{ij} q_i \geqslant p_j, j = 1, \ldots n$$

and, in particular, if strict inequality holds, the activity is not used, i.e. its level is zero. These three sets of constraints represent the conditions for a competitive equilibrium. The question remains whether a set of values can be found for the variables x_j, p_j and q_i.

The answer to this equestion is 'yes', at least as long as some basic requirements are met. The reason lies in the close similarity between the equilibrium conditions and the properties of optimal solutions to linear-programming problems. Suppose for the moment that a set of non-negative prices $p_1 \ldots p_n$ are given. Then as long as all combinations of activities require a positive input for some product j, some coefficient a_{ij} is positive for each product j and as long as the resources are all available in some quantity, however small, there will be some meaningful finite optimal solution, with at least one variable positive, for the following programming problems:

(a) find a non-negative set of values for the variables x_j to maximize

$$\sum_{j=1}^{n} p_j x_j$$

subject to $\qquad \sum_{j=1}^{n} a_{ij} x_j \leqslant r_i, i = 1, \ldots m,$

(b) find a non-negative set of values for the variables q_i to minimize

$$\sum_{i=1}^{m} r_i q_i$$

subject to $\qquad \sum_{i=1}^{m} a_{ij} q_i \geqslant p_j, j = 1, \ldots n$

These two problems are closely related and, while the first can be considered as the primal problem, the second is the dual problem. The association between the solutions of the two problems has occurred before and has been referred to as the duality. As a result, if any activity is included at a positive level the income obtained from selling the output equals the cost of inputs. If the income is less than cost, the activity is not used. Also, if there is a positive price of an input, the resources of that input are fully used while, if there is a surplus, the price will be zero. Thus the equilibrium conditions are upheld, and it remains to see whether a special set of prices can be found for which the system outputs meet demand.

There does exist such a set of prices. This was shown by R. Dorfman, P. Samuelson and R. Solow who traced relationships between sets of values for the product and resource prices. Briefly, their proof relies on starting with an initial set of values for prices $p_1 \ldots p_n$, and another for the associated demand levels. It finds a pair of linear-programming problems based on the above inequalities and objective functions, but with different prices p_j. These are chosen so that the optimal solution in terms of variables x_j is proportional to the quantities originally demanded. The argument is that, as long as the inequalities describe a convex region and the demand functions are well defined and continuous, there will always be one set of prices p_j which traces into itself, and hence provides an equilibrium solution. Further, as has been shown by A. Wald in his original studies of the system, the resultant values for the quantities and prices of the product are unique, as long as the demand functions are based on an aggregate consumer behaviour that displays the same rationality as individual consumers. If, in addition, the production activities are independent of each other with respect to their coefficients a_{ij}, then the resource prices are also uniquely determined.

One property that is a feature of duality is the coincidence of the optimal values of the objective functions of the two programming problems. Thus, for the optimum,

$$\sum_{j=1}^{n} p_j x_j^0 = \sum_{i=1}^{n} r_i q_i^0$$

and so, in equilibrium, the budget must balance. Whatever is paid for product purchases is matched by the income from resource sales. Moreover, if the competitive prices $p_1 \ldots p_n$ and resource allocations $r_1 \ldots r_m$ are given, then besides possibly violating the demand requirements, other allocations of production levels and resource prices will leave

$$\sum_{j=1}^{n} p_j x_j \geq \sum_{i=1}^{m} r_i q_i$$

This confirms that the zero profit of the producing sector is the largest that could be achieved, and so the objectives of the individual profit-maximizing firms are realized.

Linear Techniques and the Economy

What is also significant is that one of the two programming problems has an objective function which is the total productive output of the system. Perfect competition is founded on a system in which every member fights for his own position and yet the result is exactly the same as if some community goal were pursued. This goal is an optimization of output judged on the basis of competitive prices and subjected to fixed resource supplies. The competitive equilibrium is therefore efficient in terms of the best technological use of the resources.

A third interpretation of the equilibrium looks at the welfare of the consumers in a sense now attributed to V. Pareto. Bearing in mind that the demand functions f_j are derived from aggregating the quantities of products chosen by individual consumers, the discussions of Chapter 2 will require that the following conditions hold

$$\frac{\delta U_i}{\delta x_j} - \lambda_i p_j \leqslant 0, j = 1, \ldots n$$

where $U_i(x_1 \ldots x_n)$ is the utility function for any consumer i, p_j and x_j are the price and quantity of product j, and λ_i is a constant for that consumer. Therefore, if a consumer is moved slightly from one set of quantities of products by amounts $dx_j{}^i$, $j = 1, \ldots n$, the change in utility will be

$$dU_i = \sum_{j=1}^n \frac{\delta U_i}{\delta x_j} dx_j{}^i \leqslant \lambda_i \sum_{j=1}^n p_j dx_j{}^i$$

The values λ_i represent the marginal utility of income and, if consumers always look on increases in income as means of increasing satisfaction, they will be positive. Then, by dividing by λ_i and summing over all consumers,

$$\sum_{i=1}^m \frac{1}{\lambda_i} dU_i = \sum_{i=1}^m \frac{1}{\lambda_i} \sum_{j=1}^n \frac{\delta U_i}{\delta x_j} dx_j{}^i \leqslant \sum_{j=1}^n p_j dx_j$$

where dx_j is the total change in the quantity of product. As the competitive equilibrium is a maximum in terms of output, any such change will be to a worse position, i.e. the change in cost of output, and hence total weighted utility, is zero or negative,

$$\sum_{i=1}^m \frac{1}{\lambda_i} dU_i \leqslant 0$$

As all the λ_i are positive, then any reallocation in which utilities change will include one value dU_i which is negative. Hence there is no reallocation that can be made that will not be detrimental to at least one consumer. This condition is known as *Pareto optimality*.

The properties of competitive equilibria can be followed through to more general formulations. These can include the replacement of the fixed resource availability by supply functions where prices are a determinant of the quantity extracted. Further developments involve the consideration of intermediate goods as well as alternative production processes. Then the theory becomes more complex, but the general discussions still reveal similar properties.

9.3 Input–Output Analysis

A different approach and one that enables empirical studies to be made is *input–output analysis*, pioneered by W. Leontief in the late 1930s. He was concerned with the economy acting as a 'black-box' in which processes turned inputs into outputs. The productive activities again have the familiar property of constant returns to scale, and it is assumed that goods and activities can be so defined that each activity is identified by the production of one good only. Further, to begin, goods produced by different activities will be considered different.

The formulation is very similar to that used in the Walras–Cassel model. There, is, though, a division of goods into two different groups that is particularly important in the subsequent empirical use of the model. This assumes that there is only one primary good, labour. Everything else is manufactured within the economy, is used up in the production activities and is consumed by the household sector. The only exceptions are other primary goods that are allowed to be freely available, and hence do not enter the model at all. Thus, if x_j, $j = 1, \ldots n$, denotes the amount produced of non-primary goods j, and x_0 the amount of labour, then, with the economy in equilibrium, the amount produced of each item must be at least as great as that consumed, i.e.

$$x_i \geqslant \sum_{j=1}^{n} a_{ij} x_j + C_i, i = 1, \ldots n,$$

and

$$x_0 \geqslant \sum_{j=1}^{n} a_{0j} x_j$$

where a_{ij}, $i = 0, 1, \ldots n, j = 1, \ldots n$, is the amount of good i that is required in unit production of good j, and C_i is the amount of good i consumed by the household sector. As the discussions are about levels of production and consumption, the variables x_j and consumption levels C_i would be expected to be non-negative. The same assumption is made about the coefficients a_{ij}, thus effectively ruling out the possibility of joint production. This provides a second assumption important for the interpretation of data.

Linear Techniques and the Economy

The two simplifying assumptions, of one primary good and no joint production, have a direct implication about the existence of alternative production processes. So far it has been assumed that goods produced by different processes are different in the eyes of the consumer. If some were not, then a firm would clearly have the opportunity to make a choice of alternative processes to satisfy its customers and the selection would be made on the basis of current prices weighted by production coefficients. If the firm were interested in maximizing profit it would adopt the cheapest process. Thus, for a given set of prices, only one process need be operative. This is an important property, for it means that the earlier assumption of different goods from different processes is a restriction that is no longer needed. Whenever there is a potential equivalence of two goods in the way they are used by the consumers, or, in other words, *substitution*, there will emerge one dominant process that would be observed in practice. The actual process will depend on the values of the prices. The problem left is how dependent the set of current prices will be on the situation in the economy. The other assumption, of one primary factor, helps with the answer.

The significance of prices in the Leontief system can be demonstrated by turning to another pair of linear programming problems. The only input into the economy as a whole is labour, and if the overall aim of planning is to achieve consumption targets with the minimum amount of labour, then it is possible to look for a solution of the problem, minimize

$$\sum_{j=1}^{n} a_{0j} x_j$$

subject to

$$x_i \geqslant \sum_{j=1}^{n} a_{ij} x_j + C_i, i = 1, \ldots n,$$

i.e.

$$x_i - \sum_{j=1}^{n} a_{ij} x_j \geqslant C_i, i = 1, \ldots n,$$

for non-negative variables $x_j, j = 1, \ldots n$. This is the problem that would also describe a perfectly competitive equilibrium where firms attempted to maximize their profits by minimizing costs. This time, though, they would include both the cost of labour and also the cost of other goods. To see the similarity, consider the dual problem to the above minimization, namely,

maximize
$$\sum_{j=1}^{n} u_j C_j$$
subject to
$$u_j - \sum_{i=1}^{n} a_{ij} u_i \leqslant a_{0j}, j = 1, \ldots n,$$

for non-negative variables u_j. Putting the dual problem into more familiar terms with $p_j/p_0 = u_j$ it becomes
maximize
$$\sum_{j=1}^{n} p_j C_j$$
subject to
$$p_j - \sum_{i=1}^{n} a_{ij} p_i < a_{0j} p_0, j = 1, \ldots n.$$

Because of duality, the relationships between the optimal solutions to the two problems will indicate that the values p_j satisfy exactly the requirements of a perfectly competitive equilibrium of profit-maximizing firms, namely that an activity is operated when its profitability is zero, an unprofitable activity is not used, there is no surplus quantity of a good when its price is positive and prices are zero when there is a surplus. Hence the solution of minimum total cost of labour coincides with individual firms minimizing the cost of all their inputs. The equilibrium price system is denoted by the solution in terms of the variables $u_j = p_j/p_0$ for the modified dual problem. It will provide the ratios of prices p_j of goods j with the price of labour, p_0. Any set of prices proportional to these values will suit the equilibrium.

Now, if data is collected about a real competitive equilibrium which supposedly has been operating under fixed consumption targets, the only activities observed and included will be those operating at a positive level. By virtue of the duality this will mean that the whole set of prices fits into the system of equations

$$p_j - \sum_{i=1}^{n} a_{ij} p_i = a_{0j} p_0, j = 1, \ldots n.$$

As there are n linear equations in $n + 1$ variables $p_j, j = 0, 1, \ldots n$ it would be possible, for a given set of coefficients a_{ij}, to derive the price ratios p_j/p_0 by solving the simultaneous equations. This would give the relationships

$$p_j = \sum_{i=1}^{n} A_{ij} a_{0i} p_0, j = 1, \ldots n,$$

where A_{ij} are a set of coefficients derived by combining the coefficients a_{ij}. The actual combination will arise during the elimination necessary to solve the equations. Thus, once the activities that operate at a positive level have been identified, a set of perfectly competitive prices can be derived. This will help extend the discussion of alternative production processes one stage further. It starts now at the consumption targets C_i, moves to the selection of activities that will achieve those targets at minimum cost, then to the perfectly competitive prices for that allocation, and finally to the processes which the profit-maximizing firms choose.

For the systems that are likely to be observed in practice and follow the above assumptions, it can be shown that the chain from consumption targets to prices and processes always gives the same results. The competitive prices and the set of processes chosen by profit-maximizing firms are independent of the original consumption targets C_i as long as there is one primary factor, no joint production and the coefficients a_{ij} fit a number of restrictions. The coefficients will be required to satisfy what have become known as the *Hawkins–Simons conditions*, a set of conditions on the size of the coefficient values considered in varying combinations. Broadly, the requirement is that all activities should be productive, or self-sustaining. In other words, any processes will provide a positive advantage in terms of the quantities of product forthcoming when weighed against the inputs required. So, at least $a_{ii} < 1$ for all diagonal elements, $i = 1, \ldots n$. This property would be expected of an observed system which, if modelled correctly, should have no activities or groups of activities that are not self-sustaining. The main point about the conditions is that they ensure that the linear programming problem has a solution with a set of positive values for the output levels. Hence there is a solution to the simultaneous equations for prices expressing them in terms of the price of the single primary factor, labour. All goods are therefore evaluated against the same basic factor in a way independent of the target C_i.

The importance of the independence is two-fold. Firstly, it reinforces the suggestion that the problem involving minimization on a national scale of the labour input gives the same solution as the individual firms minimizing the cost of all their inputs. Whatever the targets, the same result will be achieved when the prices of all non-primary goods are traced back to the price of labour. Thus, any alternative processes that are available can be examined and selected, once and for all, according to the lowest price in terms of labour for that good. The indirect labour content of all goods will be defined and provides a measure of their cost to firms. Therefore, whether it be direct or indirect, the labour content is minimized at all levels in the economy. Secondly, the independence of selection of processes for the production of each good will mean that, if an economy is observed over different points in time when presumably different demands are made of the system, the same coefficients will apply even though there are enough alternative processes to create an effective non-linear technology. Therefore, in finding the answer to the problem about the dependence of the choice of processes, a significant point has been made about the constancy of production coefficients in observed equilibria. This is particularly important, for observations on a system can be made over time to evaluate the fixed coefficients and they can then be used for prediction. The past measurements can be projected into the future. So a theoretical remark about substitution has suggested a mechanism by which an economy's activities can be planned to achieve specific future targets.

As can be imagined the grand intentions of input–output analysis are much harder to follow in practice than to describe. The analysis is useful, though, in a number of areas, one of which has already been briefly mentioned, the establishment of data and a computational method for the inter-regional location model of Chapter 8. More usually, it is acknowledged as a method of breaking down data at a nationally aggregated level so that significant interrelationships can be drawn out between sectors of the economy. To start with, a table of money flows is constructed to indicate what value of goods has passed from one industry to the next in a given period of time. Goods are essentially measured at a set of current prices which from then on become simply a set of units of quantity. These prices need not be those of a perfectly competitive system, and industries will make actual profits or losses according to the relative total cost of inputs and the price obtained for the output. If, in addition, the industries are defined so that single outputs can be identified, then there will be the beginnings of a Leontief input–output system. The flows will essentially provide, when reduced to unit levels, a set of coefficients a_{ij} which form the basis of the production technology.

This conversion of the original flow table to an input–output table is the most difficult part of the exercise. There is considerable scope in the definition of goods, and the analyst must search for methods of simplifying the model to within the practicalities of computation and yet still retain the significant interrelationships. He will be continually faced with problems of aggregating the activities and consolidating industries to fit both his own requirements and those of the Leontief assumptions. In all, his success will be determined by his skill.

There is a final point to be pursued about the achievement of consumption targets. If they have been specified, how can the levels of production and labour be determined? The answer comes back to

Linear Techniques and the Economy

the coefficients A_{ij} again. Just as competitive prices were obtained by making profits on observable activities equal to zero, the activity levels x_j can be found by equating production to total consumption. This involves solving the simultaneous equations

$$x_i - \sum_{j=1}^{n} a_{ij}x_j = C_i, \, i = 1, \ldots n.$$

These are the same as the other equations for prices except that the array of coefficients is turned on its side and different values appear on the right-hand side. If the equations were solved it is not surprising that the result would be

$$x_i = \sum_{j=1}^{n} A_{ij}C_j, \, i = 1, \ldots n.$$

Therefore, for the labour input,

$$x_0 = \sum_{i=1}^{n} \sum_{j=1}^{n} a_{0i}A_{ij}C_j$$

Hence, for any set of non-negative target values C_j, the production plan can be found.

The coefficients A_{ij} have an interpretation in both sets of equations. They are the input–output versions of what are usually called *multipliers*, and they sum up the total contribution of one good embedded in another. Not only are the first round effects included, i.e. the contributions from the productive coefficient a_{ij}, but also the quantities that are used up indirectly. Thus second-round effects might well be included due to the quantity of good i consumed in the production of a quantity of another good k which is then used in the production of good j. In this case it would equal the product $a_{ik}a_{kj}$. So, if it were possible to trace the third, fourth and fifth rounds and so on as far as there were any quantities to think about, the total relationship between goods could be established in terms of the original coefficients. This would give the formula

$$A_{ij} = a_{ij} + \sum_{k=1}^{n} a_{ik}a_{kj} + \sum_{k=1}^{n}\sum_{l=1}^{n} a_{ik}a_{kl}a_{lj} + \ldots, \, i,j = 1, \ldots n, \, i \neq j$$

To make up the set of diagonal elements the additional formula can be given by

$$A_{ii} = 1 + a_{ii} + \sum_{k=1}^{n} a_{ik}a_{ki} + \sum_{k=1}^{n}\sum_{l=1}^{n} a_{ik}a_{kl}a_{li} + \ldots, \, i = 1, \ldots n.$$

These formulae give an alternative method of calculating the coefficients. Instead of solving the simultaneous equations, the different rounds of the production process could be traced as far as they made significant contributions to the total. The formulae also provide a detailed history of what happens to each unit of labour. The cross-product $\sum_{j=1}^{n} a_{0i}A_{ij}$ indicates exactly how much labour eventually ends up in the production of units of good j that are consumed by the household sector. It therefore helps sum up the behaviour of the 'black box' by indicating the ratio of the quantity of each good that leaves the productive sector in terms of the quantity input of the only primary good.

10 Consideration of Time

The models described in the book, from the behaviour of consumers and firms up to the operation of the economy, have concentrated on seeking a static equilibrium. Such models are already well established and lend themselves to a linear programming approach. Recently it has been repeatedly argued that the real world is far more complex than these equilibrium models indicate, and that it is with a dynamic approach that current problems should be tackled. In fact no-one would dispute the statement that a dynamic formulation of any situation is potentially more useful that a static one. It is, after all, unreasonable to assume that real world adjustments are made so quickly that consumers adopt a new expenditure pattern, firms re-tool their production lines or economies switch their resources at the drop of a hat. There are delays, or *lags*, built into the system which account for the time taken, say, for a household to come round to buying a car or a washing machine again, or for a firm to write off its current machinery. Thus changes will take time, and any system will only gradually move from one position in the general direction of an improvement. The problem is that, although lags can be incorporated in any model so creating a very impressive display of mathematics, they make calculations much more complicated. In an actual situation the delays are difficult to pinpoint and hence accurately portray inside a model. In addition, the large amount of data which would be needed before their size could be determined is difficult to collect and interpret, particularly in the areas of consumer and business decision-making. This really creates an impasse with, on the one hand, an elaborate theory which is remote from the realities of life and, on the other, a construction which appears to carry all the elements of the actual situation but in a way that is too complex to use. In fact, strictly, it makes it impossible to continue with the practical job of explanation or prediction for which a model should be used. It is only when 'reasonableness' is allowed to prevail that the deadlock is broken.

It is worth stressing at this stage that economic theory aims at explaining, in as simple a way as possible, how particular phenomena might arise. So as a first point it could be claimed that the static models help the understanding of a situation even if they do not reflect accurately all its facets. They therefore help the formulation in broad outline of future plans. From this point of view, as long as they are reasonable simplifications of reality, the models in the book are useful.

The question of prediction is more difficult, though, for there is then more opportunity for inaccuracies. Once a future target has been stipulated it is required to steer the variables towards fixed values. Essentially this can be done by predicting the effects of changes in variables over which there is direct control, the *instruments* of the situation. The problem is that the size of the effects is brought into question in relation to all other disturbances or lags that might arise. A comprehensive model is therefore required in which accuracy is emphasized, but yet there is then great scope for misrepresentation of the actual situation.

In the first place, it is possible with some systems to ignore the complications of lags or disturbances. An example is the response of peak-hour traffic to changes in a road system. Typically such systems are characterized by a quick spread of information among consumers, a weak relationship between quantity of a good and the amount of machinery or capital equipment required to produce it, a small amount of organization or administration in the actual changes, and no reliance on external phenomena that themselves alter with time. Quite simply the complexities that arise from the time element can be set to one side and an equilibrium model used.

Secondly, there is the possibility of including delays in the model at points where they are particularly meaningful. A good example is the situation facing farmers with, say, an annual crop cycle. The income gained from one year's crop will be used to buy seed for next year's. There is then a fixed delay in the investment/return cycle. Similarly, a firm might well review its investment decisions on a cyclical basis as a result of accounting within the tax year, or to coincide with a pattern of board meetings. Otherwise, it might as a matter of policy agree to review investment decisions a fixed time after they have been implemented. Either way, a delay springs up which could well create fluctuations. In fact, the field that has been given a great deal of attention is trade-cycle theory where economists have repeatedly attempted to explain the fluctuations in the economy as a whole. The questions there are of both analysis and prediction, 'where are the lags in the system?' and 'how might government intervention be used as a means of control?'.

Thirdly, if time is included in the actual plan formulation, then some of the burden can be taken away from the prediction stage and the extra detail incorporated in the actual policy. It makes the specification of the problem complicated, and so the approaches tend to be

Consideration of Time 153

highly specialized. Through the importance, though, of such dynamic planning problems to large-scale industry, the literature in the field is expanding quickly and many techniques have been developed, particularly for the scheduling of production and planning of expenditure. These topics, though, are not discussed further here, and all that is included in this chapter is a brief mention of some of those problems that link in with the previous material.

10.1 Consumer Behaviour

The book started with a look at consumer behaviour. In one of its most generalized forms this involved the maximization of a weighted sum of utility functions subject to a set of linear constraints. If the model is to be dynamic, it could well be said that the variables describe a life-long programme of purchases, and a separate utility function is created to describe the individual's tastes and preferences for each stage in his life. Similarly, the constraint could include the income levels over the same intervals of time. They could also introduce a particular feature of dynamic models, the carry-over of capital goods from one interval of time to the next.

Once a time element is introduced it is necessary to recognize the special position of capital goods. Although a large proportion of income may go into the purchase of a capital item in one year, the impact of that item remains for a longer period. Its ownership can provide benefits in subsequent years and, if it is resold, it can even provide an increase in future income. The way such goods are included in the consumer model is by interpreting purchases as changes in capital stock. Then the actual quantities of goods either enter the utility expressions directly to indicate satisfaction derived from ownership itself, or otherwise act as a constraining factor in consumption of non-capital goods. Suppose, for example, that x_{Tt} denoted the stock of television sets held by a household over a period of time t, while x_{Ct} denoted the amount of viewing time in the same period. The purchase of the sets and their later sale constitute the only changes in the variable x_{Tt} and hence are recorded in the budget constraints at the time of the transactions. The direct effect of the variable will be through satisfaction drawn from the ownership of the television. On the other hand, the cost of viewing will be derived from the cost of electricity and the wear and tear on the electronics while the set is switched on and the amount x_{Ct} of viewing will indicate the satisfaction gained from actually watching programmes. The two variables x_{Tt} and x_{Ct} will be linked through a common constraint which indicates the obvious fact that, if x_{Tt} is zero, then x_{Ct} is also zero. (This particular condition will be difficult to incorporate in a linear model. Ideally, it will be represented by the inequality

$$x_{Ct} \leqslant M\, x_{Tt}$$

where M is a very large constant, and the variable x_{Tt} is restricted to integer values. To drop the restriction to integer values would mean accepting that television sets are infinitely divisible. This is unreasonable unless the sets have different viewing facilities or they are shared between a large number of independent viewers.)

The consumer model can therefore be extended over time. The exercise, though, has remained an academic one through the difficulty coping with the intricacies of human behaviour. By way of contrast, the approach of conventional economics has been from an entirely different angle. It has looked for constancy in the proportions into which income is divided, particularly with regard to the separation of *consumption* and *savings*. (Now 'savings' means anything that is not directly consumed.) In terms of the above example this discriminates between variables x_{Ct} and x_{Tt}, and effectively aims at developing a 'rule of thumb' by which budgets can be worked out in two separate parts corresponding to the two types of expenditure.

10.2 Production Planning

The introduction of varying capital stocks is of more practical use in the production planning problems. The activity analysis framework can be applied over different periods of time and can include changes in capital stock along with the quantities of non-capital goods that are consumed. Indeed much of the success of mathematical programming has been due to its ability to cope with just this type of production plan, or programme as it might be more appropriately called. Whereas the programme choice might appear complex, the technique offers a systematic framework by which an analysis can be made.

The actual production problems will usually involve the optimization of profit, revenue, cost or capacity at a particular point in time. The courses of action will be constrained by the production technology, the mix of inputs and the capacities of the processes declared over a whole period of time. In addition, there will be stipulations about interim output levels, the flow of money in and out of the firm, and also the restrictions on storage space for goods held over from one time to the next. A situation could arise, for example, where demand varied and yet the efficiency of production depended on steady levels of operation of the processes. It would then be required to look at the trade-off between varying the production levels against storing either the inputs or outputs and thus incurring an expense both indirectly, as a result of money tied up in 'inactive' goods, and also directly, through the cost of warehousing facilities.

The difficulty with such programming problems is that, if the situation is complicated enough to warrant special techniques, it will certainly involve a large number of variables and constraints. Hence the success of an application will depend on the ability to handle computations of large size, or otherwise recognize a special form to the constraints and break down the calculations into smaller units.

10.3 Growth in the Economy

The production system in the economy as a whole is infinitely more complex than the firm, and includes a large amount of feedback both within a single time period and over successive periods. This aspect attracted a considerable amount of attention from the mathematician J. von Neumann in the 1930s. Briefly, his attention centred on a very simple production model with labour treated as a productive activity along with all other processes. The household effectively turns consumption goods into a labour output which is ploughed back into the manufacturing sector. Thus it is possible to create a closed system where all productive outputs are fed back at a later date. The time delay between a good being output and used as an input is the same throughout and is equal to one period of update of the system. If a set of time points are specified, say at yearly intervals, then questions can be phrased about the growth patterns of industrial activity as the system is updated from one point to the next. Typically, given a starting point with a set of quantities of all goods, it is required to choose from the possible outputs in the following year, and then in subsequent years, a growth pattern that is in some way preferred.

The point that interested von Neumann concerns the optimum rate of growth defined in a particular way. *Balanced growth* requires the output combination for any particular year to retain the same proportionality as the input combination. The quantities output are equal to a constant proportion of the quantities input. The initial discussions asked which set of initial quantities leads to the greatest growth rate. When chosen, the corresponding growth path has become known as the *Neumann ray*.

Subsequent studies have turned up an interesting property of the Neumann ray, that it can usually be shown to lie at the centre of the paths that provide the fastest growth. Although the basic model is particularly simple and idealized, it is still possible to ask real questions to gain an insight into more complicated problems. What is useful is to examine how quickly a specific output target can be reached given that a start is made from a given set of inputs at the base year. It can be shown that under quite general conditions, whatever the starting point or target, the most efficient growth path—i.e. the one that reaches the target first—will 'spend most of its time' following closely the Neumann ray. The inevitable analogy has followed with the Neumann ray being compared to a motorway, or 'turnpike,' and travel between two points lying at small distances off the motorway being expected to follow a path that includes the motorway for some part of the time. The analogy has branded studies of the property with the description *turnpike theorems*.

To leave the impression that growth theory is confined to the von Neumann model would be misleading. There is a large amount of conventional economics around the selection of policies for growth on the national scale, and there are a number of review articles that give good accounts of the topic.

References and Further Reading

Chapter 1

Clarkson, G. P. E. (1963) 'Interactions of Economic Theory and Operations Research' *in* Oxenfeldt, A. R. (Ed.) *Models of Markets*, Columbia University Press; *also in* Clarkson, G. P. E. (1968) *Managerial Economics*, Penguin Modern Economics.

Dorfman, R. (1960) 'Operations Research', *American Economic Review* **50**, 575–623; *also in* American Economic Association and Royal Economic Society (1968) *Surveys of Economic Theory, Vol. III, Resource Allocation*, Macmillan.

Chapter 2

Neumann, J. von and O. Morgenstern (1947) *Theory of Games and Economic Behaviour*, Princeton University Press.

Henderson, J. M. and R. E. Quandt (1958) *Microeconomic Theory; a Mathematical Approach*, McGraw-Hill (chapter 2).

Baumol, W. J. (1965) *Economic Theory and Operations Analysis*, Prentice-Hall (chapters 9, 10 and 22).

Samuelson, P. A. (1963) *Foundations of Economic Analysis*, Harvard University Press (chapters 5, 6 and 7).

Chapter 3

Dorfman, R., P. A. Samuelson and R. Solow (1958) *Linear Programming and Economic Analysis*, McGraw-Hill (chapter 6).

Baumol (1965, chapters 5, 11 and 12).

Chapter 4

Dantzig, G. B. (1951) 'Maximisation of a Linear Function of Variables subject to Linear Inequalities' *in* Koopmans, T. C. (Ed.) *Activity Analysis of Production and Allocation*, Cowles Commission Monograph No. 13.

Vajda, S. (1961) *Mathematical Programming*, Addison-Wesley (chapters 2 and 5).
Dorfman *et al.* (1958, chapters 3, 4 and 7).
Baumol (1965, chapters 5 and 6).
Dantzig, G. B. and P. Wolfe (1960) 'The Decomposition Algorithm for Linear Programming', *Operations Research* **8**, Jan., Feb., Oct.; *also in Econometrica* **9**, No. 4, 1961.
Baumol, W. J. and T. Fabian (1964) 'Decomposition, Pricing for Decentralisation, and External Economies' *Management Science* **11**, No. 1.

Chapter 5

Henderson *et al.* (1958, chapters 3, 4 and 6).
Dorfman *et al.* (1958, chapters 8, 15 and 16).
Baumol (1965, chapters 11, 12, 13 and 14).
Robinson, J. (1933) *The Economics of Imperfect Competition*, Macmillan.
Neumann, J. von, *et al.* (1947).

Chapter 6

Hitchcock, F. L. (1941) 'The Distribution of a Product from Several Sources to Numerous Localities' *Journal of Mathematics and Physics* **20**, 224–30.
Charnes, A. and W. W. Cooper (1957) 'Management Models and Industrial Applications of Linear Programming' *Management Science* **4**, 38–91; *also in* Clarkson (1968).

Chapter 7

Walter, A. A. (1961) 'The Theory and Measurement of Private and Social Cost of Highway Congestion' *Econometrica* **29**, 676–99.
Beckmann, M., C. B. Mcguire and C. B. Winsten (1956) *Studies in the Economics of Transportation*, Cowles Commission for Research in Economics, Yale University Press.
Overgaard, K. R. (1966) 'Traffic Estimation in Urban Transportation Planning' *Acta Polytechnica Scandinavica, Report 34*, Technical University of Denmark.
Ministry of Transport (1964) *Road Pricing; The Economic and Technical Possibilities*, London, Her Majesty's Stationery Office.

Chapter 8

Stevens, B. H. and E. W. Coughlin (1958) 'A Note on Inter-areal Linear Programming for a Metropolitan Region' *Journal of Regional Science* **1**, No. 2.

Herbert, J. D. and B. H. Stevens (1960) 'A Model for the Distribution of Residential Activity in Urban Areas' *Journal of Regional Science* **2**, No. 1.

Moses, L. (1960) 'A General Equilibrium Model of Production, Inter-Regional Trade and Location of Industry' *Review of Economics and Statistics* **42**, 373–97.

Chapter 9

Dorfman *et al.* (1958, chapters 9, 10 and 13).
Baumol (1965, chapter 20).
Hicks, J. R. (1968) 'Linear Theory' *in* American Economic Association *et al.* (1968).

Chapter 10

Baumol (1965, chapter 19).
Dorfman *et al.* (1958, chapters 11 and 12).
Hahn, F. H. and R. C. O. Matthews (1965) 'The Theory of Economic Growth: A Survey', *in* American Economic Association and Royal Economic Society (1965) *Surveys of Economic Theory*, Macmillan.

Appendix A
Mathematical Notes

1 A variable is denoted by a letter with optional subscripts, e.g. x_1, λ, and adopts values from a given range. When it is required to distinguish between a variable name and the value that variable takes the values are normally denoted by adding a superscript, e.g. x_1^0.

2 A mathematical function is a means of tracing from the current values of a set of variables to a new value. For example, the height, h, of a hill can be deduced from the longitude, x_1 and latitude, x_2 of a point by using a map. The process would be equivalent to calculating some complicated formula f, the details of which are unknown. This would be denoted by

$$h = f(x_1, x_2)$$

Given values of the variables x_1 and x_2, the formula f gives a unique value for the expression $f(x_1, x_2)$, and this value is passed on to the variable h.

3 If a function's variables are constrained, they restrict attention to a limited region. For example, the maximum height might be sought for all points within a field on the side of the hill. The longitude and latitude of these points will be constrained to lie within the boundary.

4 'Contours' can be drawn by examining what combinations of the variables $x_1, x_2, \ldots x_n$ give a constant value for the function $f(x_1, x_2, \ldots x_n)$. For example, contours of height λ can be denoted by all pairs of values of the variables x_1, x_2 which give the function $f(x_1, x_2)$ the value λ. By altering the value of λ different contours are described.

5 The notation '$\equiv$' can be read as 'it is a matter of definition that there is equality'.

'$\doteqdot$' can be read 'approximately equal to'
'$>$' can be read 'is greater than'
'$\geqslant$' can be read 'is greater than or equal to'
'$<$' can be read 'is less than'
'$\leqslant$' can be read 'is less than or equal to'

Appendix A

'$\sum_{j=1}^{n}$' can be read 'the sum of the following expression where the value j ranges from 1 to n, e.g.

$$\sum_{i=1}^{n} p_j x_j = p_1 x_1 + p_2 x_2 + \ldots + p_n x_n$$

'$\in$' can be read 'belonging to the set'.

It can be noted that, if for two values x' and y',

$$x' \leqslant y'$$

then also

$$-x' \geqslant -y'$$

and

$$x' - y' \leqslant 0$$

6 The function f is *concave* if, for any value s which satisfies $0 \leqslant s \leqslant 1$, and any two combinations of values $(x_1^1, x_2^1, \ldots x_n^1)$ and $(x_1^2, x_2^2, \ldots x_n^2)$ it is true that

$$f(sx_1^1 + (1-s)x_1^2, sx_2^1 + (1-s)x_2^2, \ldots, sx_n^1 + (1-s)x_n^2)$$
$$\geqslant sf(x_1^1, x_2^1, \ldots x_n^1) + (1-s)f(x_1^2, x_2^2, \ldots x_n^2).$$

An example of a concave function is the height of a well-rounded hill, where height, $h = f(x_1, x_2)$. A straight line joining two points on the surface of the hill will entirely lie inside the hill, beneath the surface. This property will not be satisfied near the base of the hill.

7 A *convex* function is the direct opposite of a concave function and the definition differs only in the $\geqslant$ sign being replaced by a $\leqslant$ sign. An example is the height of the surface of a moon crater where a line joining two points lies entirely above the surface. So if the function f is concave, the function $g \equiv -f$ is convex and vice versa.

8 A *convex region* is a continuous set of points such that a line joining any two points runs only through other points of the set. For example, the interior of an orange, or of a pyramid, is a convex region.

9 A contour $\lambda = f(x_1, x_2, \ldots x_n)$ which is drawn for a concave function f is *convex to the origin* if the value of the function at the origin is less than the value λ. It is *concave to the origin* if the value of the function is greater than the value λ. The reverse applies for a convex function.

10 If for two variables x_1 and x_2 the quantities are plotted along the axes of a graph, then each pair of values for the variables represents a point. If the values of the variables are connected by a linear relationship, e.g.

$$a_1 x_1 + a_2 x_2 = b$$

where a_1, a_2 and b are constants, then all the points represented by the value-pairs lie on a straight line. If the constants are all positive, then the line runs from 'north-west' to 'south-east' and as the constant b is increased, the line moves in a 'north-easterly' direction.

The generalization of the line $a_1 x_1 + a_2 x_2 = b$ is the *hyperplane* $a_1 x_1 + a_2 x_2 + \ldots + a_n x_n = b$. Also, the generalization of the curve $f(x_1, x_2) = \lambda$ is the *surface* $f(x_1, x_2, \ldots x_n) = \lambda$. This move to more than two dimensions means that it is difficult to visualize the geometric interpretation of the equations. Most concepts, though, carry over.

11 The notation $\mathrm{d}x$ is used to indicate a small change in the variable x. Thus the value $x^1 + \mathrm{d}x^1$ is a small increment away from the value x^1.

12 The change in value of a function from one combination of values to another close to it can be broken into a number of different parts. To move from $(x_1, x_2, \ldots x_n)$ to $(x_1 + \mathrm{d}x_1, x_2 + \mathrm{d}x_2, \ldots x_n + \mathrm{d}x_n)$ it is possible to change each variable in turn by moving in directions that keep the others constant. The slope in these directions are called the *partial derivatives*

$$\frac{\delta f}{\delta x_j}, j = 1, \ldots n.$$

Thus the *total differential*, i.e. the change in value of the complete function, is given by the near equality

$$\mathrm{d}f \doteq \frac{\delta f}{\delta x_1} \mathrm{d}x_1 + \frac{\delta f}{\delta x_2} \mathrm{d}x_2 + \ldots + \frac{\delta f}{\delta x_n} \mathrm{d}x_n$$

(Because the partial derivatives are not necessarily constant over the move, even though it is small, the total change will not be exactly equal to the sum of moves in the different directions. For the moves anticipated, however, the error in assuming equality is very small and will usually be neglected. A fuller description can be seen in the discussion of the Taylor expansion below where the discrepancy is expanded in terms of other derivatives.)

For example, a small move on the side of a hill can be interpreted as the sum of a northerly move and an easterly move. The slopes in the two directions are $\delta f/\delta x_1$ and $\delta f/\delta x_2$ respectively, and the total gain in height will equal the sum of the products of these slopes and the distances moved in each direction,

$$\mathrm{d}f = \frac{\delta f}{\delta x_1} \mathrm{d}x_1 + \frac{\delta f}{\delta x_2} \mathrm{d}x_2$$

The changes in slope may be treated similarly. Partial derivatives are themselves functions of the same variables, and so it is possible

Appendix A

to think of the partial derivatives of a partial derivative, e.g. $\delta^2 f/\delta x_j^2$, $\delta^2 f/\delta x_j \delta x_k$. In the example there were two partial derivatives and there are four second-order partial derivatives, namely

$$\frac{\delta^2 f}{\delta x_1^2}, \frac{\delta^2 f}{\delta x_1 \delta x_2}, \frac{\delta^2 f}{\delta x_2 \delta x_1}, \frac{\delta^2 f}{\delta x_2^2}.$$

The middle two are the same.

The partial derivatives when there is just one variable, e.g. $f(x)$, are called simply *derivatives*, df/dx. The total differential of a new function which is the product of two other functions is given by the following rule:

$$d(fg) = f dg + g df$$

For example, if one function is the function $f(x_1, x_2)$ and the other is simply the variable p, the total differential of the product $pf(x_1, x_2)$ is

$$d(p f(x_1, x_2)) = \frac{\delta f}{\delta x_1} p\, dx_1 + \frac{\delta f}{\delta x_2} p\, dx_2 + f(x_1, x_2)\, dp$$

13 The extreme points of a differentiable function f for which the variables are unrestricted coincide with points for which the total differential is zero however the variables are altered,

$$df = 0$$

This could be anticipated by considering again the hill. The land will be flat in the immediate vicinity of the summit and in whichever direction height is examined there will be no perceptible change for very small distances. (The error in the equality

$$df = \frac{\delta f}{\delta x_1} dx_1 + \frac{\delta f}{\delta x_2} dx_2$$

will be too small to be noticed and the slope at the actual summit is assumed to persist over the distance through which the move is made. At the summit $\delta f/\delta x_1 = \delta f/\delta x_2 = 0$ and $df = 0$).

The extreme points of a differentiable function f for which the variables are restricted by the equation set

$$g_i = 0, i = 1 \ldots m$$

where g_i are a set of differentiable functions, coincide with points for which

$$d(f - \lambda_1 g_1 - \lambda_2 g_2 - \ldots - \lambda_m g_m) = 0$$

for a set of values $\lambda_1, \lambda_2, \ldots \lambda_m$. These are known as the *Lagrange Multipliers*. For example, if the function $f(x_1, x_2) \equiv c_1 x_1 + c_2 x_2$ is to be maximized subject to

$$g(x_1, x_2) \equiv x_1^2 + x_2^2 - d^2 = 0$$

then the optimal point (x_1^0, x_2^0) would have property that

$$d(f - \lambda g) = df - \lambda dg - g d\lambda = 0$$

The changes involved in the total differentials can be in any final direction. In its most general form a move could be made so that the x_1 and x_2 variables changed their values by amounts dx_1 and dx_2. Then if it is expanded fully,

$$df - \lambda dg - g d\lambda$$
$$= \left(\frac{\delta f}{\delta x_1} dx_1 + \frac{\delta f}{\delta x_2} dx_2\right) - \lambda \left(\frac{\delta g}{\delta x_1} dx_1 + \frac{\delta g}{\delta x_2} dx_2\right) - g d\lambda$$
$$= \left(\frac{\delta f}{\delta x_1} - \lambda \frac{\delta g}{\delta x_1}\right) dx_1 + \left(\frac{\delta g}{\delta x_2} - \lambda \frac{\delta g}{\delta x_2}\right) dx_2 - g d\lambda$$

By choosing the changes along the axes, the equation gives rise to two relationships which the partial derivatives obey,

$$dx_2 = d\lambda = 0 \text{ provides } \frac{\delta f}{\delta x_1} - \lambda \frac{\delta g}{\delta x_1} = c_1 - 2\lambda x_1 = 0$$

$$dx_1 = d\lambda = 0 \text{ provides } \frac{\delta f}{\delta x_2} - \lambda \frac{\delta g}{\delta x_2} = c_2 - 2\lambda x_2 = 0$$

Any small move away from the minimum value of a convex function f will cause the value to increase at an increasing rate, i.e.

$$d^2 f \geqslant 0$$

where $d^2 f$ is the second-order total derivative. A move from the maximum value of a concave function f will similarly be associated with the condition

$$d^2 f \leqslant 0$$

For example, taking the two-variable concave function $f(x_1, x_2)$,

$$d^2 f = \frac{\delta^2 f}{\delta x_1} dx_1^2 + 2 \frac{\delta^2 f}{\delta x_1 \delta x_2} dx_1 dx_2 + \frac{\delta^2 f}{\delta x_2^2} dx_2^2 \leqslant 0$$

Appendix A

14 The values of a function f at two points can be related using a series, the sum of a progression of terms. If the function is differentiable at all points, then the relationship may be expressed by the *Taylor expansion* as follows,

$$f(x_1 + dx_1, x_2 + dx_2, \ldots x_n + dx_n)$$
$$= f(x_1, x_2, \ldots x_n) + \sum_{i=1}^{n} \frac{\delta f}{\delta x_i} dx_i + \frac{1}{2} \sum_{i=1}^{n} \sum_{j=1}^{n} \frac{\delta f}{\delta x_i \delta x_j} dx_i dx_j + \ldots$$

where the summation is continued indefinitely. If it is terminated at the rth term, then the remaining terms will, in total, still be small compared with $(dx_i)^r$ for any $i = 1, \ldots n$.

15 The *inverse of a function* $f(x)$ is another function g for which $x = g(y)$ when $y = f(x)$. For notation

$$g = f^{-1}$$

and $$g(f(x)) = f^{-1}(f(x)) = x$$

The inversion can only be carried out when the function defines a one-to-one relationship, i.e. corresponding to any value y there is only one value of x for which $y = f(x)$. It has the effect of turning the graph of the function on its side. So, if the function h is defined by the combination of two functions f_1 and f_2 so,

$$h = (f_1^{-1} + f_2^{-1})^{-1}$$

then the relationship $y = h(x)$ can be derived by putting $x = x_1 + x_2$ where $x_1 = f_1^{-1}(y)$ and $x_2 = f_2^{-1}(y)$. This defines a function which, when inverted, gives the function h.

16 If g is a function defined by differentiation of another function, i.e.

$$g(x) = \frac{df(x)}{dx},$$

then the inverse of function g is the *integral* of function g. So, where h is the integral, $h(g(x)) = x$. For notation, the integral is usually written

$$\int_{x'}^{x''} g(x) \, dx$$

which can be read 'the integral between x' and x'' of the function $g(x)$'. Suppose that the original function is plotted on a graph and that the slope df/dx of the line is measured and plotted alongside. Now the change in value of the function f between two points x' and x

can be obtained directly from comparing the function f, or indirectly by accumulating all the small changes along the curve between the same points. These small changes are reflected in the slope df/dx and it would be possible to add all the changes as they are measured in the second curve. This is what integration does and

$$f(x'') - f(x') = \int_{x'}^{x''} g(x)\, dx$$

where $g(x) \equiv df/dx$. In other words, it evaluates the area underneath the graph of the slope, $g(x)$, by weighting the values of the function g by the length of time they apply. If x' were kept constant and the integral examined up to a varying point x'', then the effect of changes in x'' would be summed up in the total derivative of the integral, i.e.

$$d(f(x'') - f(x')) = d\left(\int_{x'}^{x''} g(x)\, dx\right)$$

and, as x' is constant

$$g(x) = df(x'') = d\left(\int^{x''} g(x)\, dx\right)$$

Integration is the inverse operation to differentiation and vice versa.

Appendix B
Mathematical Programming: Summary

Typically, *mathematical programming* is concerned with finding the maximum or minimum value of some function $f(x_1, \ldots x_n)$ while there are restrictions

$$g_i(x_1, \ldots x_n) \leqslant 0, i = 1, \ldots m$$

placed on the variables. g_i are a set of functions given to the problem. (The restrictions effectively set an upper limit to the functions' values. Although the upper limits are here zero, they can be changed to any other constant value by adding that value to both sides. Equally, by multiplying through by -1 the nature of the inequalities can be reversed to denote a lower limit. As a matter of convention, though, the standard form for the restrictions will be taken as 'less than or equal to zero' conditions.)

If the functions f and g_i are linear, then the question of the optimal set of values for the variables will be a matter for *linear programming*.

1 The Kuhn–Tucker Conditions

Suppose that the functions $f(x_1, \ldots x_n)$ and $g_i(x_1, \ldots x_n), i = 1, \ldots m$, have derivatives defined at all points, and that f is concave and g_i are convex. Then the point $(x_1^0, \ldots x_n^0)$ defines a maximum of f subject to

$$g_i(x_1, \ldots x_n) \leqslant 0, i = 1, \ldots m,$$

and

$$x_j \geqslant 0, j = 1, \ldots n,$$

if and only if non-negative values $y_1^0, \ldots y_m^0$ exist which satisfy all three of the following:

$$-\frac{\delta f}{\delta x_j} + \sum_{i=1}^{m} y_i^0 \frac{\delta g_i}{\delta x_j} \geqslant 0, j = 1, \ldots n,$$

$$\sum_{i=1}^{m} \left(-\frac{\delta f}{\delta x_j} + \sum_{i=1}^{m} y_i^0 \frac{\delta g_i}{\delta x_j} \right) x_j^0 = 0$$

and

$$\sum_{i=1}^{m} g_i(x_1^0, \ldots x_n^0) y_i^0 = 0$$

The partial derivatives are evaluated at the point $(x_1^0, \ldots x_n^0)$.

As the values x_j^0 and y_i^0 are non-negative, the conditions imply that
(i) if $x_j^0 > 0$ for some j, then also

$$-\frac{\delta f}{\delta x_j} + \sum_{i=1}^{m} y_i^0 \frac{\delta g_i}{\delta x_j} = 0$$

(ii) if $y_i^0 > 0$ for some i, then also

$$g_i(x_1^0, \ldots x_n^0) = 0$$

The Kuhn–Tucker conditions can be extended to include equality constraints in the restrictions on the variables. If, say, an extra set of constraints

$$g_i(x_1, \ldots x_n) = 0, i = m+1, m+2, \ldots m'$$

were added, then extra values y_i^0, $i = m+1, m+2, \ldots m'$ would have to be included in the summations over i in the three equations. These values can be zero, positive or negative.

Another extension would be to drop the non-negative assumption on some of the variables x_j. The formulation then begins to resemble the method of Lagrange Multipliers and the conditions will require that

$$-\frac{\delta f}{\delta x_j} + \sum_{i=1}^{m} y_i^0 \frac{\delta g_i}{\delta x_j} = 0$$

for those variables x_j which can assume positive and negative values.

2 Duality

The standard linear programming problem seeks a set of values for the non-negative variables $x_1, \ldots x_n$ which maximizes

$$\sum_{j=1}^{n} c_j x_j$$

subject to the constraints

$$\sum_{j=1}^{n} a_{ij} x_j \leqslant b_i, i = 1, \ldots m,$$

Appendix B

where c_j, a_{ij} and b_i are sets of constants. This can be called the *primal problem*.

There is an associated problem, the *dual*, which requires a set of values of the non-negative variables $y_1, \ldots y_m$ which minimizes

$$\sum_{i=1}^{m} b_i y_i$$

subject to the constraints

$$\sum_{i=1}^{m} a_{ij} y_i \geqslant c_j, j = 1, \ldots n$$

The relationship between the primal and dual problems can be summarized as follows: in one case the objective function is maximized, in the other minimized. In one there are 'less than or equal to' signs, in the other 'greater than or equal to'. Also, the objective function coefficients of one are the constraint stipulations of the other and vice versa, and the array of constraint coefficients is turned on its side as the first problem is changed to the second.

The principle of duality infers a number of relationships between any pair of optimal solutions $(x_1^0, \ldots x_n^0)$ and $(y_1^0, \ldots y_m^0)$:

$$x_j^0 > 0 \text{ implies} \sum_{i=1}^{m} a_{ij} y_i^0 = c_j, j = 1, \ldots n,$$

$$\sum_{i=1}^{m} a_{ij} y_i^0 > c_j \text{ implies } x_j^0 = 0, j = 1, \ldots n,$$

$$y_i^0 > 0 \text{ implies} \sum_{j=1}^{n} a_{ij} x_j^0 = b_i, i = 1, \ldots m,$$

and $\sum_{j=1}^{n} a_{ij} x_j^0 < b_i \text{ implies } y_i^0 = 0, i = 1, \ldots m.$

Also,

$$\sum_{j=1}^{n} c_j x_j^0 = \sum_{i=1}^{m} b_i y_i^0$$

If one of the original variables x_j, is not constrained to be non-negative then the corresponding dual constraint will be an equality, i.e.

$$\sum_{i=1}^{m} a_{ij} y_i^0 = c_j$$

Similarly, if one of the original constraints were a strict equality, i.e.

$$\sum_{j=1}^{n} a_{ij}x_j^0 = b_i$$

then the corresponding dual variable will not be constrained to be non-negative.

If the Kuhn–Tucker conditions are applied to the optimum of the primal problem, then there exists an associated set of non-negative values for which

$$-c_j + \sum_{i=1}^{m} y_i^0 a_{ij} \geq 0, j = 1, \ldots, n,$$

$$\sum_{j=1}^{n} \left(-c_j + \sum_{i=1}^{m} y_i^0 a_{ij} \right) x_j^0 = 0$$

and

$$\sum_{i=1}^{m} \left(\sum_{j=1}^{n} a_{ij}x_j^0 - b_i \right) y_i^0 = 0$$

These values are solutions to the dual problem. Moreover, all solutions to the dual problem satisfy the conditions.

The optimal values of the dual variables are the Simplex multipliers corresponding to the optimal solution of the primal problem, and vice versa.

Index

Accounts, breakdown of, 52, 57
Activity analysis, 32
Activity table, 33
Algorithm
  decomposition, 58
  Simplex, 42
Analysis
  activity, 32
  input–output, 135, 144
Approach
  macroscopic, 2
  microscopic, 2

Balanced growth, 155
Ballot system, 108
Basic feasible solution, 32
Basic solution, 32
Basic variables, 44
Baskets, market, 130
Beckmann, M., 116
Behaviour
  consumer, 4, 5
  of the firm, 65
  rational, 6
Bid system, 107
Bundle, 130

Capital goods, 153
Cardinal utility, 5
Cassel, G., 139
Commuter patterns, 88, 104, 105
Competition
  imperfect, 66
  monopolistic, 67, 81
  perfect, 66, 68
  pure, 65
Concave
  functions, 161
  to the origin (curve), 161
Conditions
  Hawkins–Simons, 147
  Kuhn–Tucker, 15, 167
Constant returns to scale, 30, 138

Constant–sum game, 81
Constraints, redundant, 32
Consumer surplus, 107, 119
Consumption, 154
Contours, 160
Convex
  functions, 161
  region, 30, 161
  to the origin (curve), 161
Corner rule, north–west, 93
Cost
  generalized, 113
  shadow, 93
Coughlin, E. W., 126
Curves
  demand, 11, 13, 66
  indifference, 5
  supply, 47, 66

Dantzig, G. B., 42, 62
Decomposition, 58
  algorithm, 58
Degenerate solution, 93, 102
Degrees of freedom, 31
Demand curves, 11, 13, 66
Dependent variables, 38
Derivatives, 163
  partial, 162
Diet problem, 19
Differential, total, 163
Dorfman, R., 142
Dual problem, 141, 169
Duality, 86, 141, 168
Dynamic models, 151

Economic rent, 123, 125
Economics, 2
  normative, 3, 123
  positive, 3, 123
Economies of scale, 30, 77
Effect
  income, 13
  substitution, 13, 14

Entrepreneur, 25
Equations, first-order homogeneous, 71
Equilibrium
  general, 139
  stable, 67
  unstable, 67
Expansion, Taylor, 165
Expected pay-off, 84
Explanation (model), 2

Feasible combination, 11
Feasible region, 27
Feasible solution, basic, 32
Final goods, 139
First-order homogeneous equations, 71
Freedom, degrees of, 31
Function
  inverse of a, 165
  objective, 27
  production, 25
  utility, 5
Functions, 160
  concave, 161
  convex, 161

Game, constant-sum, 81
Games, market, 80
General equilibrium, 139
Generalized cost, 113
Goods
  final, 139
  intermediate, 139
  primary, 139
Gravitation, law of (commuter patterns), 105
Growth, balanced, 155

Hawkins–Simons conditions, 147
Herbert, J. D., 129
Homogeneous equations, first-order, 71
Hyperplane, 162

Imperfect competition, 66
Imputed valuations, 52, 58, 75, 95
Imputed value, net, 56
Income
  effect, 13
  marginal utility of, 19, 143
Independent variables, 31
Indifference curves, 5
Indifference map, 5
Indifference surfaces, 5

Input–output analysis, 135, 144
Inputs, 25
Instruments, 152
Integral, 165
Intermediate goods, 139

Kuhn–Tucker conditions, 15, 167

Lagrange Multipliers, 164, 168
Lags, 151
Law of diminishing marginal utility, 7
Law of gravitation (commuter patterns), 105
Leontief, W., 144
Linear problem, 30
Linear programming, 167
Long-term planning, 25

Macroscopic approach, 2
Map, indifference, 5
Marginal rate of substitution, 6, 7
Marginal revenue, 53
Marginal utility of income, 19, 143
Market games, 80
Market research, 4
Master program (decomposition), 62
Mathematical programming, 2, 167
Maxi–min strategy, 82
Mcguire, C. B., 116
Method
  pivotal, 46
  Simplex, 32, 42
Microscopic approach, 2
Mini–max strategy, 82
Ministry of Transport, 118
Mixed strategy, 82, 84
Model, 2
Models
  dynamic, 86, 151
  static, 86, 151
Money value of effect of price change, 13
Monopolistic competition, 67, 80
Monopoly, 65, 77
Morgenstern, O., 6
Moses, L., 133
Multipliers, 149
  Lagrange, 164, 168
  Simplex, 55, 170

Net inputed value, 56
Neumann, J. von, 5, 155
Neumann ray, 155
Non-basic variables, 44

Index

Non-linear production, 77
Normative economics, 3, 123
North-west corner rule, 93
Nutrition problem, 19

Objective function, 27
Oligopoly, 67
Operations research, 1
Optimal point, 15, 31
Optimality, Pareto, 143
Ordinal utility, 5
Origin
  concave to the, 161
  convex to the, 161
Outputs, 25

Pareto, V., 143
Pareto optimality, 143
Partial derivatives, 162
Pay-off
  expected, 84
  matrix, 81
Penn-Jersey Transportation Study, 129
Perfect competition, 66, 68
Perfectly operating markets, 66
Pivot, 46
  column, 46
  row, 46
Pivotal method, 46
Planning
  long-term, 25
  production, 26
  short-term, 25
  urban, 88, 104
Positive economics, 3, 123
Prediction (model), 2
Pricing, road, 118
Primal problem, 141, 169
Primary goods, 139
Problem
  dual, 141, 169
  primal, 141, 169
  transportation, 89, 123, 135
Production
  function, 25
  planning, 26
Profit, 65, 72
Programming
  linear, 167
  mathematical, 2, 167
Pure competition, 65

Rational behaviour, 6
Redundant constraints, 32
Region
  convex, 30, 161
  feasible, 27
Rent, economic, 123, 125
Research, market, 4
Returns to scale
  constant, 30, 138
  variable, 77
Revenue, marginal, 53
Road pricing, 118

Samuelson, P., 142
Saving, 130
Savings, 154
Scale
  constant returns to, 30, 138
  economies of, 30, 77
  variable returns to, 77
Shadow costs, 93
Short-term planning, 25
Simplex method, 32, 42
Simplex multipliers, 55, 170
Slack variables, 35
Solow, R., 142
Solution
  basic, 32
  basic feasible, 32
  degenerate, 93, 102
Stable equilibrium, 67
Static model, 86, 151
Stevens, B. H., 126, 129
Strategy, 82
  maxi-min, 82
  mini-max, 82
  mixed, 82, 84
Substitution, 103, 145
  effect, 13, 14
  marginal rate of, 6, 7
Supply curve, 47, 66
Surface, 162
Surfaces, indifference, 5
Surplus consumer, 107, 119

Table, activity, 33
Taylor expansion, 165
Total differential, 163
Traffic assignment, 117
Transport, Ministry of, 118
Transportation problem, 89, 123, 135
Transportation study, 116
Transportation Study, Penn-Jersey, 129
Turnpike theorems, 156

Unstable equilibrium, 67
Urban planning, 88, 104
Utility
  cardinal, 5
  function, 5
  law of diminishing marginal, 7
  of income, marginal, 19, 143
  ordinal, 5

Valuations
  at the margin, 52
  imputed, 52, 58, 75, 95
Value
  money effect of price change, 13
  net imputed, 56

Variable returns to scale, 77
Variables, 160
  basic, 44
  dependent, 38
  independent, 31
  non-basic, 44
  slack, 35
Vertex, 31

Wald, A., 142
Walras, L., 138, 139
Winsten, C. B., 116
Wolfe, P., 62